0058191

W9-BKK-415

3 1702 00030 1771

WILCGOV99

Congressional government

To his father, the patient guide of his youth, the gracious companion of his manhood, his best instructor and most lenient critic, this book is affectionately dedicated by the author.

Congressional government

A study in American politics
by WOODROW WILSON

Introduction by WALTER LIPPMANN

GLOUCESTER, MASS.

PETER SMITH

1973

A MERIDIAN BOOK

Published by The World Publishing Company
2231 West 110th Street, Cleveland 2, Ohio

First Meridian printing February 1956
Seventh printing March 1963

Introduction by Walter Lippmann copyright © 1956
by The World Publishing Company.
Originally published 1885.
Library of Congress Catalog Card Number: 56-6567
Printed in the United States of America   7WP363

Reprinted, 1973, by Permission of
World Publishing
Times Mirror

ISBN: 0-8446-3187-6

Contents

Contents

Introduction by WALTER LIPPMANN

Woodrow Wilson wrote this book in 1883 and 1884. When he reread it in 1900 (in order to do a preface to the fifteenth printing), he had such serious misgivings about it that he warned his readers new developments "may put this whole volume hopelessly out of date." Soon thereafter he thought they had, and in 1908 he wrote another book, his *Constitutional Government in the United States,* to supersede it. In this second book are the main ideas which Wilson took with him to the White House in 1912.

The basic difference between the first book and the second is in the conception of the power of the President. When Wilson was writing his *Congressional Government,* he supposed that Congress was necessarily the central and predominant power in the American system, and that the Presidency had become an ineffectual office. But at the turn of the century and after the war with Spain and America's entrance into world politics, he took a radically opposite view: the President was again, as in the early days of the Republic, "at the front of affairs." * It was because the center of power had moved from one end of Pennsylvania Avenue to the other that Wilson thought this book was out of date.

And so it was if we judge the book as Wilson himself al-

* See below, Preface to the Fifteenth Edition.

7

ways judged it—as an attempt to describe realistically how the American constitutional system works. The fact is that at times the system works as he describes it in this book and at other times it works as he describes it in the second book. For what he did in this first book was to give a clinical description of a disease, not permanent but recurrent, to which the system is subject. With the fresh eye of genius, and with the intuitions of a man who is born to govern, he described the breakdown of government in the aftermath of the Civil War. The book deals with the American system in the twenty dangerous and humiliating years between the death of Lincoln and the rise of Grover Cleveland. It is the first analytical description of what happens when the President is weak and helpless, of how power and responsibility disintegrate when the members of Congress, and more specifically their standing committees, are predominant. Some of the factual details are no longer correct. But the morbid symptoms which he identified are still clearly recognizable when the disease recurs, and there is a relapse into Congressional supremacy. This was a good book to read during the Harding Administration. It is a good book to have read at the end of the Truman and at the beginning of the Eisenhower Administrations. It is one to be taken to heart by all who have seen the ravages of McCarthyism.

Woodrow Wilson was a graduate student at Johns Hopkins University when in the summer of 1884 he finished writing this book. He was then twenty-eight years old. After an unhappy year of trying without much success to practice law in Atlanta, he had returned, as if from exile, to the academic life. He had escaped from the "dreadful drudgery" of the law office, he had become engaged to Ellen Axson, he was no longer "buried in humdrum life down . . . in slow, ignorant, uninteresting Georgia," and he was able again to satisfy his "passion for original work . . . to become a master of philosophical discourse, to become capable and apt in instructing as great a number of persons as possible." His "plain necessity," he wrote to his friend, Heath Dabney,[1] was "some profession which will afford me a moderate support, favorable conditions for study, and considerable leisure; what better can I be, therefore, than a professor, a lecturer upon subjects whose study most delights me?"

This book was his first work after he had come to his decision to give up the law and to go into teaching. But he did not mean to stay there. It is evident enough from his letter to Dabney that he thought of teaching as a way station, as a means of earning a living, of having the leisure to study political philosophy and history, and of preparing himself for his true vocation in the great world. His true vocation was political leadership. He had had no doubts about that since his undergraduate days at Princeton. In the terms of his Presbyterian doctrine he had since then known himself to be a predestined and foreordained agent who was being "guided by an intelligent power outside himself." So sure was he of his vocation that in his senior year at Princeton he had entered into "a solemn covenant" with his friend and classmate, Charles Talcott. Some four years later when he went to Johns Hopkins, he remembered the covenant. In a letter[2] written to Ellen Axson, shortly after they became engaged, he wrote that Talcott and he had pledged themselves that "we would school all our powers and passions for the work of establishing the principles we held in common; that we would acquire knowledge that we might have power; and that we would drill ourselves in all the arts of persuasion, but especially in oratory . . . that we might have facility in leading others into our ways of thinking and enlisting them in our purposes."

The covenant with his friend Charles Talcott bears upon the general feeling and animus of this book. The young Wilson believed that the American constitutional system is radically defective and that it should be made over on the British model. For Congressional government, as he describes it in this book, offers nothing but misery and frustration to the kind of public man that Wilson was preparing himself to be. He aspired to acquire power because he could shape opinion by his oratory, and under Congressional government it was in the standing committees that power was traded and manipulated.

It is interesting, I think, that ambitious as he was and dedicated to a political career, the young Wilson seems never to have aspired to be President. That was not because he thought the Presidency was too high for him. It was because he saw that power, which was what he cared about, was in Congress. The ambition of the young Wilson was to be a Senator from Virginia,[3] and he prepared himself for his destiny by making himself, through much practice, into an effective orator. He believed that as Congress was the predominant power in the American system, oratory was, or rather that oratory should be, the means of leading Congress. In the English system, as Wilson supposed it to be, governments were made and were unmade in Parliament by the great orators, like Gladstone.

By the age of twenty-two, in the year 1879, when he was still a senior at Princeton, Wilson had reached the main ideas with which he started when he came to write this book. They are to be found in an article which was published in the *International Review* for August, 1879. (The editor, curiously enough, who accepted this article, was his great future adversary, Henry Cabot Lodge.) The article is entitled *Cabinet Government in the United States.*[4] A responsible cabinet, he argued, was the remedy for Congressional Government—for that "despotic authority wielded under the forms of free government" by "our national Congress . . . a despotism which uses its power with all the caprice, all the scorn for settled policy, all the wild unrestraint which marked the methods of other tyrants as hateful to freedom."

When we ask ourselves why it did not occur to him to look to presidential leadership for a remedy, we must remember the times in which he was living. Wilson was a Southerner, born in Staunton, Virginia, on December 28, 1856. He had spent his boyhood in Augusta, Georgia, where his family moved when he was an infant. After the Civil War, the family went to South Carolina, where his father, Dr. Joseph Ruggles Wilson, became professor of theology in the seminary at Columbia. Wilson had grown up amidst the ruins of the Civil War and in the tragic aftermath of the Reconstruction. He was nine years old when Lincoln died. The presidents during his lifetime had been Andrew Johnson, General Grant, and Rutherford B. Hayes, whose title was clouded, and they were followed by Garfield and Chester Arthur. It was from these Presidents that Wilson drew the conclusion, which was decisive for the constitutional theory of his nonage, that the presidential office is insignificant. He was disgusted with the contemporary political scene: "eight words contain the sum of the present degradation of our political parties," he wrote, "no leaders, no principles; no principles, no parties." [5]

In England, particularly in the England of Gladstone, whose portrait Wilson had hung over his desk, he saw what he missed at home. He read Green's *Short History of the English People,* and he found it had for him an "overmastering charm." [6] He became convinced that the history of the English people is also the history of the American people. In this mood he read Walter Bagehot's *The English Constitution,* presumably in the American edition, which was published in February, 1877.

The American edition contained Bagehot's introduction to the second English edition. It is dated June 29, 1872. The whole book, but particularly, I would say, this introduction had a decisive influence on Wilson's thinking, and Wilson acknowledged it when he was working on his *Congressional Government.* In a letter[7] to Ellen Axson he wrote that "it is my purpose to show as well as I can our constitutional system as it looks in operation. My desire and ambition are to treat the American Constitution as Mr. Bagehot (do you remember Mr. Bagehot, about whom I talked to you one night on the veranda at Asheville?) has treated the English Constitution. . . . He brings to the work a fresh and original method which has made the British system much more intelligible to ordinary men than it was before, and which, if it could be successfully applied to the exposition of our federal constitution, would result in something like a revelation to those who are still reading *The Federalist* as an authoritative constitutional manual."

But it was not only Bagehot's "fresh and original method" which inspired Wilson. He had become Bagehot's disciple, and he adopted, as his own, Bagehot's critique of the American constitution.[8] This critique was written in 1872 and in the light of the quarrel between President Andrew Johnson and the Congress. Bagehot said that after Lincoln's assassination "the characteristic evils of the presidential system were shown most conspicuously . . . at the moment of all their history when it was most important to them to collect and concentrate all the strength and wisdom of their policy on the pacification of the South, that policy was divided by a strife in the last degree unseemly and degrading." In one principal respect, Bagehot went on to say, "the English system" of parliamentary government is "by far the best . . . in each stage of a public transaction there is a discussion . . . the public assists at this discussion . . . it can, through Parliament, turn out an administration which is not doing as it likes, and can put in an administration which will do as it likes. But the character of a Presdential government is, in a multitude of cases, that there is no such discussion; that when there is a discussion the fate of the government does not turn upon it and, therefore, the people do not attend to it."

The young Wilson, oppressed by the spectacle of American politics, was ready to be convinced that for the reasons given by Bagehot the English system was better than the American. The American Congress was predominant. But it governed without genuine debate. Its power, which was divided among the standing committees, was not accountable to the opinion of the nation. No one spoke for the nation. Except for Lincoln, whom he admired but who, in his view, had ignored the Constitution, there had been no President in his lifetime who represented the national interest and could cope with the overriding power of the many standing committees of Congress. So the young Wilson concluded that the normal and permanent American system had come to be what it had been in his lifetime.

If that was the American system, then drastic changes would be necessary in it. For Congressional Government, which Wilson described fearlessly and faithfully in his book, was intolerably bad government. Wilson never doubted that for good government there must be a strong Executive. If the office of President had fallen irrevocably from that "first estate of dignity" [9] which it had among the Founding Fathers, then the remedy for the radical defect of the system would lie in making a strong executive out of a responsible cabinet.

This had been, as I have been saying, Wilson's view since his Princeton days. In fact, just as he was starting to write this book, he had published in the *Overland Monthly* for January, 1884, an article called *Committee or Cabinet Government.* It concludes with a paragraph saying that "Committee Government [which Wilson used as another name for Congressional Government] is too clumsy and too clandestine a system to last. Other methods of government must sooner or later be sought, a different economy established. First or last, Congress must be organized in conformity with what is now the prevailing legislative practice of the world. English precedent and the world's fashion must be followed in the institution of Cabinet Government in the United States." [10]

But during the summer of 1884, while he was, in fact, finishing the manuscript of this book, Wilson began to undergo a fundamental change in his conception of the American system. Something happened then which caused him to refrain from mentioning the drastic reform—namely Cabinet Government on the British model—which he had advocated publicly shortly before. In the book the analysis of the evils of Congressional Government still points towards Cabinet Government as the remedy. But Wilson was no longer willing, as he was a year before, to draw that conclusion. "I am pointing out facts," he says in his book, "diagnosing, not prescribing remedies." [11]

Wilson's biographer, Mr. Ray Stannard Baker, does not deal with the question why, as he was finishing *Congressional Government,* Wilson decided not to put forth the remedy which, when he started to write, he had put forward as something that "must" be applied. Yet this was a critical turning point in Wilson's development—a turning away from the constitutional notions of his nonage, and towards those which he acted upon when he became President. If I might hazard a guess, it would be to suggest that what caused him to see the problem of Congressional Government in a new light was the rise of Grover Cleveland.

Cleveland was running for President in that summer of 1884

when Wilson was finishing his book. Now Cleveland was the first American public man in Wilson's own lifetime who aroused his interest in the office of President. He admired Cleveland and hoped ardently for his election. This may, then, have been why in that summer of 1884 he was no longer so sure that the remedy for the evils of Congressional Government was reform on the English precedent. In Cleveland for the first time in his own experience he discerned the possibility that the office of President might be restored to that "first estate of dignity" from which it had "fallen" since "the early Presidents."

I must warn the reader that there is no hard fact known to me, no letter of Wilson's, for example, which supports my hypothesis that he was influenced by the candidacy of Cleveland. It may be a mere coincidence. But it is true that until that summer Wilson had always supposed that contemporary presidents "should wear a clean and irreproachable insignificance," [12] that Congress was necessarily "predominant over its so-called coordinated branches." [13] Since Congress "has virtually taken into its own hands all the substantial powers of government," [14] the only way to create a strong executive was on the English precedent: to vest the executive power in a cabinet chosen as a committee of the Congress.

Soon after that he was no longer prepared to prescribe the remedy. If it was the appearance of Cleveland that caused him to doubt the need for the remedy, it is also true that the remedy belonged to the upper layers of his mind, not to the main body of his thinking. It was something he had borrowed, not something he had worked out by his own labor. He seems not to have paid much attention to the practical question of how so radical an alteration was to be brought about. As far as I know, Wilson's only published words on how to initiate the English system are in the article, *Committee or Cabinet Government*,[15] which appeared in the *Overland Monthly* for January, 1884.

It would be necessary, he wrote, to amend Section 6 of Article I of the Constitution so as to permit members of Congress to hold offices as members of the Cabinet . . . It would be necessary to extend the term of the President beyond four years . . . and the term of the Representatives beyond two years . . . All in all Wilson devoted less than two pages to the ways and means of carrying out the reform, and he concluded rather hastily that "the admission of members of Congress to seats in the Cabinet would be the only change of principle called for by the new order of things." [16] He appears to have assumed that the President would have a long term and would become a kind of republican monarch, the head of the state, but no longer the Chief Executive. Apparently for no better reason than that he did not think much about it, Wilson did not regard this revolutionary change in the Presidency as "a change of principle."

The truth, I believe, is that while Wilson's description of the evils of Congressional Government was deeply perceived and carefully studied from the living realities, the remedy of Cabinet Government on the English precedent was taken from a little reading. He adopted the remedy on faith when he was an undergraduate at Princeton. He continued to advocate it, though in very general terms, for a few years after that. But there is nothing to show that he had studied the English system as he was studying the American, or that he took into account how much the American social order differed from the British—that he asked himself, for example, what was the role of the Crown and of the peerage and of hereditary rank in the operation of the English system. His attachment to the reform was superficial, and that was why he ceased to advocate it as soon as the advent of Cleveland gave him reason to hope that the American system might, after all, be "self-adjusting." [17]

Wilson in his own life knew the American constitutional system in three different phases. The first was the post-Civil War era of a predominant Congress and insignificant presidents. It ended with the rise of Cleveland in the Presidential campaign of 1884. *Congressional Government* belongs to that period.

The second phase included Wilson's rise as President of Princeton University, as Governor of New Jersey, and as President of the United States, and goes on until his fall in the political disaster of 1918. This second phase was an era of strong presidents, of Cleveland, Theodore Roosevelt, and Wilson himself. The book which reflects his constitutional theories in that period is *Constitutional Government in the United States*. In it, writing four years before he ran for President, Wilson declared that "the President is at liberty, both in law and conscience, to be as big a man as he can . . . he cannot escape being leader of his party" being "the only party nominee for whom the whole nation votes . . . he is also the political leader of the nation, or has it in his choice to be . . . his is the only national voice in affairs. Let him once win the admiration and confidence of the country, and no other single force can withstand him, no combination of forces will easily overpower him. . . . His office is anything he has the sagacity and force to make it." [18]

The third phase, of which Wilson did not see the end, began with the mid-term elections of 1918. It lasted until the advent of Franklin D. Roosevelt in 1933. It was another period of Congressional Government.

Wilson died in 1924, and in this third period he was a sick and broken man. But had he retained his intellectual energy, he would have come back, I believe, to his first book. He would have come back to revise it, but also to recognize its deep insight. In revising it, he might, perhaps have taken a new view of the balance of powers in the original Constitution. Growing up, as he did, in a time when the balance had been radically turned towards Congress and against the Executive, he seems to have supposed that the balance could not be righted. The experience of his own life had shown, however, that the balance can be righted. It had shown also that it is not a stable balance, that the tendency of the system is to become unbalanced—and especially after wars when Congress is, for a time, predominant.

There exists, one might say in limbo, a third book describing the American system in its ups and in its downs. That book, alas, Woodrow Wilson was never allowed to write. But in that book he could have brought together into one field of theory the truth of his *Congressional Government* and the truth of his *Constitutional Government*. Then he would have accounted for his own rebellion as a young man, for the disaster and his defeat at the end of his life, and for the great middle years of his power and of his triumphs and of his enduring fame.

WALTER LIPPMANN

August 5, 1955

PREFACE TO FIFTEENTH PRINTING

I have been led by the publication of a French translation of this little volume to read it through very carefully, for the first time since its first appearance. The re-reading has convinced me that it ought not to go to another impression without a word or two by way of preface with regard to the changes which our singular system of Congressional government has undergone since these pages were written.

I must ask those who read them now to remember that they were written during the years 1883 and 1884, and that, inasmuch as they describe a living system, like all other living things subject to constant subtle modifications, alike of form and of function, their description of the government of the United States is not as accurate now as I believe it to have been at the time I wrote it.

This is, as might have been expected, more noticeable in matters of detail than in matters of substance. There are now, for example, not three hundred and twenty-five, but three hundred and fifty-seven members in the House of Representatives; and that number will, no doubt, be still further increased by the reapportionment which will follow the census of the present year. The number of committees in both Senate and House is constantly on the increase. It is now usually quite sixty in the House, and in the Senate more than forty. There has been a still further addition to the number of the "spend-

19

ing" committees in the House of Representatives, by the sub-division of the powerful Committee on Appropriations. Though the number of committees in nominal control of the finances of the country is still as large as ever, the tendency is now towards a concentration of all that is vital in the business into the hands of a few of the more prominent, which are most often mentioned in the text. The auditing committees on the several departments, for example, have now for some time exercised little more than a merely nominal oversight over executive expenditures.

Since the text was written, the Tenure of Office Act, which sought to restrict the President's removal from office, has been repealed; and even before its repeal it was, in fact, inoperative. After the time of President Johnson, against whom it was aimed, the party in power in Congress found little occasion to insist upon its enforcement; its constitutionality was doubtful, and it fell into the background. I did not make sufficient allowance for these facts in writing the one or two sentences of the book which refer to the Act.

Neither did I give sufficient weight, I now believe, to the powers of the Secretary of the Treasury. However minutely bound, guided, restricted by statute, his power has proved at many a critical juncture in our financial history—notably in our recent financial history—of the utmost consequence. Several times since this book was written, the country has been witness to his decisive influence upon the money markets, in the use of his authority with regard to the bond issues of the government and his right to control the disposition of the funds of the Treasury. In these matters, however, he has exercised, not political, but business power. He has helped the markets as a banker would help them. He has altered no policy. He has merely made arrangements which would release money for use and facilitate loan and investment. The country feels safer when an experienced banker, like Mr. Gage, is at the head of the Treasury, than when an experienced politician is in charge of it.

All these, however, are matters of detail. There are matters of substance to speak of also.

It is to be doubted whether I could say quite so confidently now as I said in 1884 that the Senate of the United States faithfuly represents the several elements of the nation's make-up, and furnishes us with a prudent and normally constituted moderating and revising chamber. Certainly vested interests have now got a much more formidable hold upon the Senate than they seemed to have sixteen years ago. Its political character also has undergone a noticeable change. The tendency seems to be to make of the Senate, instead of merely a smaller and more deliberate House of Representativs, a body of successful party managers. Still, these features of its life may be temporary, and may easily be exaggerated. We do not yet know either whether they will persist, or, should they persist, whither they will lead us.

A more important matter—at any rate, a thing more concrete and visible—is the gradual integration of the organization of the House of Representatives. The power of the Speaker has of late years taken on new phases. He is now, more than ever, expected to guide and control the whole course of business in the House,—if not alone, at any rate through the instrumentality of the small Committee on Rules, of which he is chairman. That committee is expected not only to reformulate and revise from time to time the permanent Rules of the House, but also to look closely to the course of its business from day to day, make its programme, and virtually control its use of its time. The committee consists of five members; but the Speaker and the two other members of the committee who represent the majority in the House determine its action; and its action is allowed to govern the House. It in effect regulates the precedence of measures. Whenever occasion requires, it determines what shall, and what shall not, be undertaken. It is like a steering ministry,—without a ministry's public responsibility, and without a ministry's right to speak for both houses. It is a private piece of party machinery within the single chamber for which it acts. The Speaker himself—not as a member of the Committee on Rules, but by the exercise of his right to "recognize" on the floor—undertakes to determine very absolutely what bills individual members shall be allowed to bring to a vote, out of the regular order fixed by the rules or arranged by the Committee on Rules.

This obviously creates, in germ at least, a recognized and sufficiently concentrated leadership within the House. The country is beginning to know that the Speaker and the Committee on Rules must be held responsible in all ordinary seasons for the success or failure of the session, so far as the House is concerned. The congressional caucus has fallen a little into the background. It is not often necessary to call it together, except when the majority is impatient or recalcitrant under the guidance of the Committee on Rules. To this new leadership, however, as to everything else connected with committee government, the taint of privacy attaches. It is not leadership upon the open floor, avowed, defended in public debate, set before the view and criticism of the country. It integrates the House alone, not the Senate; does not unite the two houses in policy; affects only the chamber in which there is the least opportunity for debate, the least chance that responsibility may be properly and effectively lodged and avowed. It has only a very remote and partial resemblance to genuine party leadership.

Much the most important change to be noticed is the result of the war with Spain upon the lodgment and exercise of power within our federal system: the greatly increased power and opportunity for constructive statesmanship given the President, by the plunge into international politics and into the administration of distant dependencies, which has been that war's most striking and momentous consequence. When foreign affairs play a prominent part in the politics and policy of a nation, its Executive must of necessity be its guide: must utter every initial judgment, take every first step of action, supply the information upon which it is to act, suggest and in large measure control its conduct. The President of the United States is now, as of course, at the front of affairs, as no president, except Lincoln, has been since the first quarter of the nineteenth century, when the foreign relations of the new nation had first to be adjusted. There is no trouble now about getting the President's speeches printed and read, every word. Upon his choice, his character, his experience hang some of the most weighty issues of the future. The government of dependencies must be largely in his hands. Interesting things may come out of the singular change.

For one thing, new prizes in public service may attract a new order of talent. The nation may get a better civil service, because of the sheer necessity we shall be under of organizing a service capable of carrying the novel burdens we have shouldered.

It may be, too, that the new leadership of the Executive, inasmuch as it is likely to last, will have a very far-reaching effect upon our whole method of government. It may give the heads of the executive departments a new influence upon the action of Congress. It may bring about, as a consequence, an integration which will substitute statesmanship for government by mass meeting. It may put this whole volume hopelessly out of date.

WOODROW WILSON

PRINCETON UNIVERSITY, 15 *August,* 1900.

PREFACE

The object of these essays is not to exhaust criticism of the government of the United States, but only to point out the most characteristic practical features of the federal system. Taking Congress as the central and predominant power of the system, their object is to illustrate everything Congressional. Everybody has seen, and critics without number have said, that our form of national government is singular, possessing a character altogether its own; but there is abundant evidence that very few have seen just wherein it differs most essentially from the other governments of the world. There have been and are other federal systems quite similar, and scarcely any legislative or administrative principle of our Constitution was young even when that Constitution was framed. It is our legislative and administrative *machinery* which makes our government essentially different from all other great governmental systems. The most striking contrast in modern politics is not between presidential and monarchical governments, but between Congressional and Parliamentary governments. Congressional government is Committee government; Parliamentary government is government by a responsible Cabinet Ministry. These are the two principal types which present themselves for the instruction of the modern student of the practical in politics: administration by semi-independent executive agents who obey the dictation of a legislature to which they are not responsible, and administration by executive agents who are the accredited leaders and accountable servants of a legislature virtually supreme in all things. My chief aim in these essays has been, therefore, an adequate illustrative contrast of these two types of government, with a view to making as plain as possible the actual conditions of federal administration. In short, I offer, not a commentary, but an outspoken presentation of such cardinal facts as may be sources of practical suggestion.

WOODROW WILSON

JOHNS HOPKINS UNIVERSITY, *October* 7, 1884.

ONE

*The laws reach but a very little way. Constitute government how you please, infinitely the greater part of it must depend upon the exercise of powers, which are left at large to the prudence and uprightness of ministers of state. Even all the use and potency of the laws depends upon them. Without them your commonwealth is no better than a scheme upon paper; and not a living, active, effective organization.—*BURKE.

*The great fault of political writers is their too close adherence to the forms of the system of state which they happen to be expounding or examining. They stop short at the anatomy of institutions, and do not penetrate to the secret of their functions.—*JOHN MORLEY.

INTRODUCTORY

It would seem as if a very wayward fortune had presided over the history of the Constitution of the United States, inasmuch as that great federal charter has been alternately violated by its friends and defended by its enemies. It came hard by its establishment in the first place, prevailing with difficulty over the strenuous forces of dissent which were banded against it. While its adoption was under discussion the voices of criticism were many and authoritative, the voices of opposition loud in tone and ominous in volume, and the Federalists finally triumphed only by dint of hard battle against foes, formidable both in numbers and in skill. But the victory was complete,—astonishingly complete. Once established, the new government had only the zeal of its friends to fear. Indeed, after its organization very little more is heard of the party of opposition; they disappear so entirely from politics that one is inclined to think, in looking back at the party history of that time, that they must have been not only conquered but converted as well. There was well-nigh universal acquiescence in the new order of things. Not everybody, indeed, professed himself a Federalist, but everybody conformed to federalist practice. There were jealousies and bickerings, of course, in the new Congress of the Union, but no party lines, and the differences which caused the constant brewing and breaking of storms in Washington's first cabinet were of personal rather than of political import. Hamilton and Jefferson did not draw apart because the one had been an ardent and the other only a lukewarm friend of the Constitution, so much as because they were so different in natural bent and temper that they would have been like to disagree and come to drawn points wherever or however brought into contact. The one had inherited warm blood and a bold sagacity, while in the other a negative philosophy ran suitably through cool veins. They had not been meant for yoke-fellows.

There was less antagonism in Congress, however, than in the cabinet; and in none of the controversies that did arise was there shown any serious disposition to quarrel with the Constitution itself; the contention was as to the obedience to be rendered to its provisions. No one threatened to withhold his allegiance, though there soon began to be some exhibition of a disposition to confine obedience to the letter of the new commandments, and to discountenance all attempts to do what was not plainly written in the tables of the law. It was recognized as no longer fashionable to say aught against the principles of the Constitution; but all men could not be of one mind, and political parties began to take form in antagonistic schools of constitutional construction. There straightway arose two rival sects of political Pharisees, each professiong a more perfect conformity and affecting greater "ceremonial cleanliness" than the other. The very men who had resisted with might and main the adoption of the Constitution became, under the new division of parties, its champions, as sticklers for a strict, a rigid, and literal construction.

They were consistent enough in this, because it was quite

natural that their one-time fear of a strong central government should pass into a dread of the still further expansion of the power of that government, by a too loose construction of its charter; but what I would emphasize here is not the motives or the policy of the conduct of parties in our early national politics, but the fact that opposition to the Constitution as a constitution, and even hostile criticism of its provisions, ceased almost immediately upon its adoption; and not only ceased, but gave place to an undiscriminating and almost blind worship of its principles, and of that delicate dual system of sovereignty, and that complicated scheme of double administration which it established. Admiration of that one-time so much traversed body of law became suddenly all the vogue, and criticism was estopped. From the first, even down to the time immediately preceding the war, the general scheme of the Constitution went unchallenged; nullification itself did not always wear its true garb of independent state sovereignty, but often masqueraded as a constitutional right; and the most violent policies took care to make show of at least formal deference to the worshipful fundamental law. The divine right of kings never ran a more prosperous course than did this unquestioned prerogative of the Constitution to receive universal homage. The conviction that our institutions were the best in the world, nay more, the model to which all civilized states must sooner or later conform, could not be laughed out of us by foreign critics, nor shaken out of us by the roughest jars of the system.

Now there is, of course, nothing in all this that is inexplicable, or even remarkable; any one can see the reasons for it and the benefits of it without going far out of his way; but the point which it is interesting to note is that we of the present generation are in the first season of free, outspoken, unrestrained constitutional criticism. We are the first Americans to hear our own countrymen ask whether the Constitution is still adapted to serve the purposes for which it was intended; the first to entertain any serious doubts about the superiority of our own institutions as compared with the systems of Europe; the first to think of remodeling the administrative machinery of the federal government, and of forcing new forms of responsibility upon Congress.

The evident explanation of this change of attitude towards the Constitution is that we have been made conscious by the rude shock of the war and by subsequent developments of policy, that there has been a vast alteration in the conditions of government; that the checks and balances which once obtained are no longer effective; and that we are really living under a constitution essentially different from that which we have been so long worshiping as our own peculiar and incomparable possession. In short, this model government is no longer conformable with its own original pattern. While we have been shielding it from criticism it has slipped away from us. The noble charter of fundamental law given us by the Convention of 1787 is still our Constitution; but it is now our *form of government* rather in name than in reality, the form of the Constitution being one of nicely adjusted, ideal balances, whilst the actual form of our present government is simply a scheme of congressional supremacy. National legislation, of course, takes force now as at first from the authority of the Constitution; but it would be easy to reckon by the score acts of Congress which can by no means be squared with that great instrument's evident theory. We continue to think, indeed, according to long-accepted constitutional formulæ, and it is still politically unorthodox to depart from old-time phraseology in grave discussions of affairs; but it is plain to those who look about them that most of the commonly received opinions concerning federal constitutional balances and administrative arrangements are many years behind the actual practices of the government at Washington, and that we are farther than most of us realize from the times and the policy of the framers of the Constitution. It is a commonplace observation of historians that, in the development of constitutions, names are much more persistent than the functions upon which they were originally bestowed; that institutions constantly undergo essential alterations of character, whilst retaining the names conferred upon them in their first estate; and the history of our own Constitution is but another illustration of this universal principle of institutional change. There has been a constant growth of legislative and administrative practice, and a steady accretion of precedent in the management of federal affairs, which have broadened the sphere and altered the functions of the government without perceptibly affecting the vocabulary of our constitutional language. Ours is, scarcely less than the British, a living and fecund system. It does not, indeed, find its rootage so widely in the hidden soil of unwritten law; its tap-root at least is the Constitution; but the Constitution is now, like Magna Carta and the Bill of Rights, only the sap-centre of a system of government vastly larger than the stock from which it has branched,—a system some of whose forms have only very indistinct and rudimental beginnings in the simple substance of the Constitution, and which exercises many functions apparently quite foreign to the primitive properties contained in the fundamental law.

The Constitution itself is not a complete system; it takes none but the first steps in organization. It does little more than lay a foundation of principles. It provides with all possible brevity for the establishment of a government having, in several distinct branches, executive, legislative, and judicial powers. It vests executive power in a single chief magistrate, for whose election and inauguration it makes carefully definite provision, and whose privileges and prerogatives it defines with succinct clearness; it grants specifically enumerated powers of legislation to a representative Congress, outlining the organization of the two houses of that body and definitely providing for the election of its members, whose number it regulates and the conditions of whose choice it names; and it establishes a Supreme Court with ample authority of constitutional interpretation, prescribing the manner in which its judges shall be appointed and the conditions of their official tenure. Here the Constitution's work of organization ends, and the fact that it attempts nothing more is its chief strength. For it to go beyond elementary provisions would be to lose elasticity and adaptability. The growth of the nation and the consequent development of the governmental system would snap asunder a constitution which could not adapt itself to the new conditions of an advancing society. If it could not stretch itself to the measure of the times, it must be thrown off and left behind, as a by-gone device; and there can, therefore, be no question that our Constitution has proved lasting because of its simplicity.

It is a corner-stone, not a complete building; or, rather, to return to the old figure, it is a root, not a perfect vine.

The chief fact, therefore, of our national history is that from this vigorous tap-root has grown a vast constitutional system,—a system branching and expanding in statutes and judicial decisions, as well as in unwritten precedent; and one of the most striking facts, as it seems to me, in the history of our politics is, that that system has never received complete and competent critical treatment at the hands of any, even the most acute, of our constitutional writers. They view it, as it were, from behind. Their thoughts are dominated, it would seem, by those incomparable papers of the "Federalist," which, though they were written to influence only the voters of 1788, still, with a strange, persistent longevity of power, shape the constitutional criticism of the present day, obscuring much of that development of constitutional practice which has since taken place. The Constitution in operation is manifestly a very different thing from the Constitution of the books. "An observer who looks at the living reality will wonder at the contrast to the paper description. He will see in the life much which is not in the books; and he will not find in the rough practice many refinements of the literary theory." [1] It is, therefore, the difficult task of one who would now write at once practically and critically of our national government to escape from theories and attach himself to facts, not allowing himself to be confused by a knowledge of what that government was intended to be, or led away into conjectures as to what it may one day become, but striving to catch its present phases and to photograph the delicate organism in all its characteristic parts exactly as it is today; an undertaking all the more arduous and doubtful of issue because it has to be entered upon without guidance from writers of acknowledged authority.

The leading inquiry in the examination of any system of government must, of course, concern primarily the real depositaries and the essential machinery of power. There is always a centre of power: where in this system is that centre? in whose hands is self-sufficient authority lodged and through what agencies does that authority speak and act? The answers one gets to these and kindred questions from authoritative manuals of constitutional exposition are not satisfactory, chiefly because they are contradicted by self-evident facts. It is said that there is no single or central force in our federal scheme; and so there is not in the federal *scheme,* but only a balance of powers and a nice adjustment of interactive checks, as all the books say. How is it, however, in the practical conduct of the federal government? In that, unquestionably, the predominant and controlling force, the centre and source of all motive and of all regulative power, is Congress. All niceties of constitutional restriction and even many broad principles of constitutional limitation have been overridden, and a thoroughly organized system of congressional control set up which gives a very rude negative to some theories of balance and some schemes for distributed powers, but which suits well with convenience, and does violence to none of the principles of self-government contained in the Constitution.

This fact, however, though evident enough, is not on the surface. It does not obtrude itself upon the observation of the world. It runs through the undercurrents of government, and takes shape only in the inner channels of legislation and administration which are not open to the common view. It can be discerned most readily by comparing the "literary theory" of the Constitution with the actual machinery of legislation, especially at those points where that machinery regulates the relations of Congress with the executive departments, and with the attitude of the houses towards the Supreme Court on those occasions, happily not numerous, when legislature and judiciary have come face to face in direct antagonism. The "literary theory" is distinct enough; every American is familiar with the paper pictures of the Constitution. Most prominent in such pictures are the ideal checks and balances of the federal system, which may be found described, even in the most recent books, in terms substantially the same as those used in 1814 by John Adams in his letter to John Taylor. "Is there," says Mr. Adams, "a constitution upon record more complicated with balances than ours? In the first place, eighteen states and some territories are balanced against the national government. . . . In the second place, the House of Representatives is balanced against the Senate, the Senate against the House. In the third place, the executive authority is, in some degree, balanced against the legislative. In the fourth place, the judicial power is balanced against the House, the Senate, the executive power, and the state governments. In the fifth place, the Senate is balanced against the President in all appointments to office, and in all treaties. . . . In the sixth place, the people hold in their hands the balance against their own representatives, by biennial . . . elections. In the seventh place, the legislatures of the several states are balanced against the Senate by sextennial elections. In the eighth place, the electors are balanced against the people in the choice of the President. Here is a complicated refinement of balances, which, for anything I recollect, is an invention of our own and peculiar to us." [2]

All of these balances are reckoned essential in the theory of the Constitution; but none is so quintessential as that between the national and the state governments; it is the pivotal quality of the system, indicating its principal, which is its federal characteristic. The object of this balance of thirty-eight States "and some territories" against the powers of the federal government, is also of several of the other balances enumerated, is not, it should be observed, to prevent the invasion by the national authorities of those provinces of legislation by plain expression or implication reserved to the States,—such as the regulation of municipal institutions, the punishment of ordinary crimes, the enactment of laws of inheritance and of contract, the erection and maintenance of the common machinery of education, and the control of other such like matters of social economy and every-day administration,—but to check and trim national policy on national questions, to turn Congress back from paths of dangerous encroachment on middle or doubtful grounds of jurisdiction, to keep sharp, when it was like to become dim, the line of demarcation between state and federal privilege, to readjust the weights of jurisdiction whenever either state or federal scale threatened to kick the beam. There never was any great likelihood that the national government would care to take from the States their plainer prerogatives, but there was always a violent probability that it would here and there steal a march over the borders where territory like its own invited it to appropriation; and it was for a mutual defense of such border-land that the two governments were given the right to call a halt upon one another. It was purposed to guard not against revolution, but against unrestrained exercise of questionable powers.

The extent to which the restraining power of the States was relied upon in the days of the Convention, and of the adoption of the Constitution, is strikingly illustrated in several of the best known papers of the "Federalist"; and there is no better means of realizing the difference between the actual and the ideal constitutions than this of placing one's self at the point of view of the public men of 1787-89. They were disgusted with the impotent and pitiable Confederation, which could do nothing but beg and deliberate; they longed to get away from the selfish feuds of "States dissevered, discordant, belligerent," and their hopes were centred in the establishment of a strong and lasting union, such as could secure that concert and facility of common action in which alone there could be security and amity. They were, however, by no means sure of being able to realize their hopes, contrive how they might to bring the States together into a more perfect confederation. The late colonies had but recently become compactly organized, self-governing States, and were standing somewhat stiffly apart, a group of consequential sovereignties, jealous to maintain their blood-bought prerogatives, and quick to distrust any power set above them, or arrogating to itself the control of their restive wills. It was not to be expected that the sturdy, self-reliant, masterful men who had won independence for their native colonies, by passing through the flames of battle, and through the equally fierce fires of bereavement and financial ruin, would readily transfer their affection and allegiance from the new-made States, which were their homes, to the federal government, which was to be a mere artificial creation, and which could be to no man as his home government. As things looked then, it seemed idle to apprehend a too great diminution of state rights: there was every reason, on the contrary, to fear that any union that could be agreed upon would lack both vitality and the ability to hold its ground against the jealous self-assertion of the sovereign commonwealths of its membership. Hamilton but spoke the common belief of all thinking men of the time when he said: "It will always be far more easy for the state governments to encroach upon the national authorities than for the national government to encroach upon the state authorities"; and he seemed to furnish abundant support for the opinion, when he added, that "the proof of this proposition turns upon the greater degree of influence which the state governments, if they administer their affairs uprightly and prudently, will generally possess over the people; a circumstance which, at the same time, teaches us that there is an inherent and intrinsic weakness in all federal constitutions, and that too much pains cannot be taken in their organization to give them all the force that is compatible with the principles of liberty." [3]

Read in the light of the present day, such views constitute the most striking of all commentaries upon our constitutional history. Manifestly the powers reserved to the States were expected to serve as a very real and potent check upon the federal government; and yet we can see plainly enough now that this balance of state against national authorities has proved, of all constitutional checks, the least effectual. The proof of the pudding is the eating thereof, and we can nowadays detect in it none of that strong flavor of state sovereignty which its cooks thought they were giving it. It smacks, rather, of federal omnipotence, which they thought to mix in only in very small and judicious quantities. "From the nature of the case," as Judge Cooley says, "it was impossible that the powers reserved to the States should constitute a restraint upon the increase of federal power, to the extent that was at first expected. The federal government was necessarily made the final judge of its own authority, and the executor of its own will, and any effectual check to the gradual amplification of its jurisdiction must therefore be found in the construction put by those administering it upon the grants of the Constitution, and in their own sense of constitutional obligation. And as the true line of division between federal and state powers has, from the very beginning, been the subject of contention and of honest differences of opinion, it must often happen that to advance and occupy some disputed ground will seem to the party having the power to do so a mere matter of constitutional duty." [4]

During the early years of the new national government there was, doubtless, much potency in state will; and had federal and state powers then come face to face, before Congress and the President had had time to overcome their first awkwardness and timidity, and to discover the safest walks of their authority and the most effectual means of exercising their power, it is probable that state prerogatives would have prevailed. The central government, as every one remembers, did not at first give promise of a very great career. It had inherited some of the contempt which had attached to the weak Congress of the Confederation. Two of the thirteen States held aloof from the Union until they could be assured of its stability and success; many of the other States had come into it reluctantly, all with a keen sense of sacrifice, and there could not be said to be any very widespread or undoubting belief in its ultimate survival. The members of the first Congress, too, came together very tardily, and in no very cordial or confident spirit of coöperation; and after they had assembled they were for many months painfully embarrassed, how and upon what subjects to exercise their new and untried functions. The President was denied formal precedence in dignity by the Governor of New York, and must himself have felt inclined to question the consequence of his official station, when he found that amongst the principal questions with which he had to deal were some which concerned no greater things than petty points of etiquette and ceremonial; as, for example, whether one day in the week would be sufficient to receive visits of compliment, "and what would be said if he were sometimes to be seen at quiet tea-parties." [5] But this first weakness of the new government was only a transient phase in its history, and the federal authorities did not invite a direct issue with the States until they had had time to reckon their resources and to learn facility of action. Before Washington left the presidential chair the federal government had been thoroughly organized, and it fast gathered strength and confidence as it addressed itself year after year to the adjustment of foreign relations, to the defense of the western frontiers, and to the maintenance of domestic peace. For twenty-five years it had no chance to think of those questions of internal policy which, in later days, were to tempt it to stretch its constitutional jurisdiction. The establishment of the public credit, the revival of commerce, and the encouragement of industry; the conduct, first, of a heated controversy, and finally of an unequal war with England; the avoidance, first, of too much love, and afterwards of too violent hatred of France; these and other like questions of great pith and moment gave it too much to do to leave it time to think of nice points of constitutional theory affecting its relations with the States.

But still, even in those busy times of international controversy, when the lurid light of the French Revolution outshone all others, and when men's minds were full of those ghosts of '76, which took the shape of British aggressions, and could not be laid by any charm known to diplomacy,—even in those times, busy about other things, there had been premonitions of the unequal contest between state and federal authorities. The purchase of Louisiana had given new form and startling significance to the assertion of national sovereignty, the Alien and Sedition Laws had provoked the plain-spoken and emphatic protests of Kentucky and Virginia, and the Embargo had exasperated New England to threats of secession.

Nor were these open assumptions of questionable prerogatives on the part of the national government the most significant or unequivocal indications of an assured increase of federal power. Hamilton, as Secretary of the Treasury, had taken care at the very beginning to set the national policy in ways which would unavoidably lead to an almost indefinite expansion of the sphere of federal legislation. Sensible of its need of guidance in those matters of financial administration which evidently demanded its immediate attention, the first Congress of the Union promptly put itself under the direction of Hamilton. "It is not a little amusing," says Mr. Lodge, "to note how eagerly Congress, which had been ably and honestly struggling with the revenue, with commerce, and with a thousand details, fettered in all things by the awkwardness inherent in a legislative body, turned for relief to the new secretary." [6] His advice was asked and taken in almost everything, and his skill as a party leader made easy many of the more difficult paths of the new government. But no sooner had the powers of that government begun to be exercised under his guidance than they began to grow. In his famous Report on Manufactures were laid the foundations of that system of protective duties which was destined to hang all the industries of the country upon the skirts of the federal power, and to make every trade and craft in the land sensitive to every wind of party that might blow at Washington; and in his equally celebrated Report in favor of the establishment of a National Bank, there was called into requisition, for the first time, that puissant doctrine of the "implied powers" of the Constitution which has ever since been the chief dynamic principle in our constitutional history. "This great doctrine, embodying the principle of liberal construction, was," in the language of Mr. Lodge, "the most formidable weapon in the armory of the Constitution; and when Hamilton grasped it he knew, and his opponents felt, that here was something capable of conferring on the federal government powers of almost any extent." [7] It served first as a sanction for the charter of the United States Bank,—an institution which was the central pillar of Hamilton's wonderful financial administration, and around which afterwards, as then, played so many of the lightnings of party strife. But the Bank of the United States, though great, was not the greatest of the creations of that lusty and seductive doctrine. Given out, at length, with the sanction of the federal Supreme Court,[8] and containing, as it did, in its manifest character as a doctrine of legislative prerogative, a very vigorous principle of constitutional growth, it quickly constituted Congress the dominant, nay, the irresistible, power of the federal system, relegating some of the chief balances of the Constitution to an insignificant rôle in the "literary theory" of our institutions.

Its effect upon the status of the States in the federal system was several-fold. In the first place, it clearly put the constitutions of the States at a great disadvantage, inasmuch as there was in them no like principle of growth. Their stationary sovereignty could by no means keep pace with the nimble progress of federal influence in the new spheres thus opened up to it. The doctrine of implied powers was evidently both facile and irresistible. It concerned the political discretion of the national legislative power, and could, therefore, elude all obstacles of judicial interference; for the Supreme Court very early declared itself without authority to question the legislature's privilege of determining the nature and extent of its own powers in the choice of means for giving effect to its constitutional prerogatives, and it has long stood as an accepted canon of judicial action, that judges should be very slow to oppose their opinions to the legislative will in cases in which it is not made demonstrably clear that there has been a plain violation of some unquestionable constitutional principle, or some explicit constitutional provision. Of encroachments upon state as well as of encroachments upon federal powers, the federal authorities are, however, in most cases the only, and in all cases the final, judges. The States are absolutely debarred even from any effective defense of their plain prerogatives, because not they, but the national authorities, are commissioned to determine with decisive and unchallenged authoritativeness what state powers shall be recognized in each case of contest or of conflict. In short, one of the privileges which the States have resigned into the hands of the federal government is the all-inclusive privilege of determining what they themselves can do. Federal courts can annul state action, but state courts cannot arrest the growth of congressional power.[9]

But this is only the doctrinal side of the case, simply its statement with an "if" and a "but." Its practical issue illustrates still more forcibly the altered and declining status of the States in the constitutional system. One very practical issue has been to bring the power of the federal government home to every man's door, as, no less than his own state government, his immediate over-lord. Of course every new province into which Congress has been allured by the principle of implied powers has required for its administration a greater or less enlargement of the national civil service, which now, through its hundred thousand officers, carries into every community of the land a sense of federal power, as the power of powers, and fixes the federal authority, as it were, in the very habits of society. That is not a foreign but a familiar and domestic government whose officer is your next-door neighbor, whose representatives you deal with every day at the post-office and the custom-house, whose courts sit in your own State, and send their own marshals into your own county to arrest your own fellow-townsman, or to call you yourself by writ to their witness-stands. And who can help respecting officials whom he knows to be backed by the authority and even by the power of the whole nation, in the performance of the duties in which he sees them every day engaged? Who does not feel that the marshal represents a greater power than the sheriff does, and that it is more dangerous to molest a mail-carrier than to knock down a policeman? This personal contact of every citizen with the federal government,—a contact which makes him feel himself a citizen of a greater state than that which controls his everyday contracts and probates his father's will,—more than offsets his sense of dependent loyalty to local authorities by creating a sensible bond of allegiance to what presents itself unmistakably as the greater and more sovereign power.

In most things this bond of allegiance does not bind him oppressively nor chafe him distressingly; but in some things it is drawn rather painfully tight. Whilst federal postmasters are valued and federal judges unhesitatingly obeyed, and whilst very few people realize the weight of customs-duties, and as few, perhaps, begrudge license taxes on whiskey and tobacco, everybody eyes rather uneasily the federal supervisors at the polls. This is preëminently a country of frequent elections, and few States care to increase the frequency by separating elections of state from elections of national functionaries. The federal supervisor, consequently, who oversees the balloting for congressmen, practically superintends the election of state officers also; for state officers and congressmen are usually voted for at one and the same time and place, by ballots bearing in common an entire "party ticket"; and any authoritative scrutiny of these ballots after they have been cast, or any peremptory power of challenging those who offer to cast them, must operate as an interference with state no less than with federal elections. The authority of Congress to regulate the manner of choosing federal representatives pinches when it is made thus to include also the supervision of those state elections which are, by no implied power even, within the sphere of federal prerogative. The supervisor represents the very ugliest side of federal supremacy; he belongs to the least liked branch of the civil service; but his existence speaks very clearly as to the present balance of powers, and his rather hateful privileges must, under the present system of mixed elections, result in impairing the self-respect of state officers of election by bringing home to them a vivid sense of subordination to the powers at Washington.

A very different and much larger side of federal predominance is to be seen in the history of the policy of internal improvements. I need not expound that policy here. It has been often enough mooted and long enough understood to need no explanation. Its practice is plain and its persistence unquestionable. But its bearings upon the status and the policies of the States are not always clearly seen or often distinctly pointed out. Its chief results, of course, have been that expansion of national functions which was necessarily involved in the application of national funds by national employees to the clearing of inland water-courses and the improvement of harbors, and the establishment of the very questionable precedent of expending in favored localities moneys raised by taxation which bears with equal incidence upon the people of all sections of the country; but these chief results by no means constitute the sum of its influence. Hardly less significant and real, for instance, are its moral effects in rendering state administrations less self-reliant and efficient, less prudent and thrifty, by accustoming them to accepting subsidies for internal improvements from the federal coffers; to depending upon the national revenues, rather than upon their own energy and enterprise, for means of developing those resources which it should be the special province of state administration to make available and profitable. There can, I suppose, be little doubt that it is due to the moral influences of this policy that the States are now turning to the common government for aid in such things as education. Expecting to be helped, they will not help themselves. Certain it is that there is more than one State which, though abundantly able to pay for an educational system of the greatest efficiency, fails to do so, and contents itself with imperfect temporary makeshifts because there are immense surpluses every year in the national treasury which, rumor and unauthorized promises say, may be distributed amongst the States in aid of education. If the federal government were more careful to keep apart from every strictly local scheme of improvement, this culpable and demoralizing state policy could scarcely live. States would cease to wish, because they would cease to hope, to be stipendiaries of the government of the Union, and would address themselves with diligence to their proper duties, with much benefit both to themselves and to the federal system. This is not saying that the policy of internal improvements was either avoidable, unconstitutional, or unwise, but only that it has been carried too far; and that, whether carried too far or not, it must in any case have been what it is now seen to be, a big weight in the federal scale of the balance.

Still other powers of the federal government, which have so grown beyond their first proportions as to have marred very seriously the symmetry of the "literary theory" of our federal system, have strengthened under the shadow of the jurisdiction of Congress over commerce and the maintenance of the postal service. For instance, the Supreme Court of the United States has declared that the powers granted to Congress by the Constitution to regulate commerce and to establish post-offices and post-roads "keep pace with the progress of the country and adapt themselves to new developments of times and circumstances. They extend from the horse with its rider to the stage-coach, from the sailing vessel to the steamer, from the coach and the steamer to the railroad, and from the railroad to the telegraph, as these new agencies are successively brought into use to meet the demands of increasing population and wealth. They are intended for the government of the business to which they relate, at all times and under all circumstances. As they were intrusted to the general government for the good of the nation, it is not only the right but the duty of Congress to see to it that the intercourse between the States and the transmission of intelligence are not obstructed or unnecessarily encumbered by state legislation." [10] This emphatic decision was intended to sustain the right of a telegraph company chartered by one State to run its line along all post-roads in other States, without the consent of those States, and even against their will; but it is manifest that many other corporate companies might, under the sanction of this broad opinion, claim similar privileges in despite of state resistance, and that such decisions go far towards making state powers of incorporation of little worth as compared with federal powers of control.

Keeping pace, too, with this growth of federal activity, there has been from the first a steady and unmistakable growth of nationality of sentiment. It was, of course, the weight of war which finally and decisively disarranged the balance between state and federal powers; and it is obvious that many of the most striking manifestations of the tendency towards centralization have made themselves seen since the war. But the history of the war is only a record of the triumph of the principle of national sovereignty. The war was inevitable, because that principle grew apace; and the war ended as it did, because that principle had become predominant. Accepted at first simply because it was imperatively necessary, the union of form and of law had become a union of sentiment, and was destined to be a union of institutions. That sense of national unity and community of destiny which Hamilton had sought to foster, but which was feeble in his day of long distances and tardy inter-communication, when the nation's pulse was as slow as the stage-coach and the postman, had become strong enough to rule the continent when Webster died. The war between the States was the supreme and final struggle between those forces of disintegration which still remained in the blood of the body politic and those other forces of health, of union and amalgamation, which had been gradually building up that body in vigor and strength as the system passed from youth to maturity, and as its constitution hardened and ripened with advancing age.

The history of that trenchant policy of "reconstruction," which followed close upon the termination of the war, as at once its logical result and significant commentary, contains a vivid picture of the altered balances of the constitutional system which is a sort of exaggerated miniature, falling very little short of being a caricature, of previous constitutional tendencies and federal policies. The tide of federal aggression probably reached its highest shore in the legislation which put it into the power of the federal courts to punish a state judge for refusing, in the exercise of his official discretion, to impanel Negroes in the juries of his court,[11] and in those statutes which gave the federal courts jurisdiction over offenses against state laws by state officers.[12] But that tide has often run very high, and, however fluctuating at times, has long been well-nigh irresistible by any dykes of constitutional state privilege; so that Judge Cooley can say without fear of contradiction that "The effectual checks upon the encroachments of federal upon state power must be looked for, not in state power of resistance, but in the choice of representatives, senators, and presidents holding just constitutional views, and in a federal supreme court with competent power to restrain all departments and all officers within the limits of their just authority, so far as their acts may become the subject of judicial cognizance." [13]

Indeed it is quite evident that if federal power be not altogether irresponsible, it is the federal judiciary which is the only effectual balance-wheel of the whole system. The federal judges hold in their hands the fate of state powers, and theirs is the only authority that can draw effective rein on the career of Congress. If their power, then, be not efficient, the time must seem sadly out of joint to those who hold to the "literary theory" of our Constitution. By the word of the Supreme Court must all legislation stand or fall, so long as law is respected. But, as I have already pointed out, there is at least one large province of jurisdiction upon which, though invited, and possibly privileged to appropriate it, the Supreme Court has, nevertheless, refused to enter, and by refusing to enter which it has given over all attempt to guard one of the principal, easiest, and most obvious roads to federal supremacy. It has declared itself without authority to interefere with the *political discretion* of either Congress or the President, and has declined all effort to constrain these its coördinate departments to the performance of any, even the most constitutionally imperative act.[14] "When, indeed, the President exceeds his authority, or usurps that which belongs to one of the other departments, his orders, commands, or warrants protect no one, and his agents become personally responsible for their acts. The check of the courts, therefore, consists in their ability to keep the executive within the sphere of his authority by refusing to give the sanction of law to whatever he may do beyond it, and by holding the agents or instruments of his unlawful action to strict accountability." [15] But such punishment, inflicted not directly upon the chief offender but vicariously upon his agents, can come only after all the harm has been done. The courts cannot forestall the President and prevent the doing of mischief. They have no power of initiative; they must wait until the law has been broken and voluntary litigants have made up their pleadings; must wait nowadays many months, often many years, until those pleadings are reached in the regular course of clearing a crowded docket.

Besides, in ordinary times it is not from the executive that the most dangerous encroachments are to be apprehended. The legislature is the aggressive spirit. It is the motive power of the government, and unless the judiciary can check it, the courts are of comparatively little worth as balance-wheels in the system. It is the subtile, stealthy, almost imperceptible encroachments of policy, of political action, which constitute the precedents upon which additional prerogatives are generally reared; and yet these are the very encroachments with which it is hardest for the courts to deal, and concerning which, accordingly, the federal courts have declared themselves unauthorized to hold any opinions. They have naught to say upon questions of policy. Congress must itself judge what measures may legitimately be used to supplement or make effectual its acknowledged jurisdiction, what are the laws "necessary and proper for carrying into execution" its own peculiar powers, "and all other powers vested by" the "Constitution in the government of the United States, or in any department or officer thereof." The courts are very quick and keen-eyed, too, to discern prerogatives of political discretion in legislative acts, and exceedingly slow to undertake to discriminate between what is and what is not a violation of the spirit of the Constitution. Congress must wantonly go very far outside of the plain and unquestionable meaning of the Constitution, must bump its head directly against all right and precedent, must kick against the very pricks of all well-established rulings and interpretations, before the Supreme Court will offer it any distinct rebuke.

Then, too, the Supreme Court itself, however upright and irreproachable its members, has generally had and will undoubtedly continue to have a distinct political complexion, taken from the color of the times during which its majority was chosen. The bench over which John Marshall presided was, as everybody knows, staunchly and avowedly federalist in its view; but during the ten years which followed 1835 federalist justices were rapidly displaced by Democrats, and the views of the Court changed accordingly. Indeed it may truthfully be said that, taking our political history "by and large," the constitutional interpretations of the Supreme Court have changed, slowly but none the less surely, with the altered relations of power between the national parties. The Federalists were backed by a federalist judiciary; the period of democratic supremacy witnessed the triumph of democratic principles in the courts; and republican predominance has driven from the highest tribunal of the land all but one representative of democratic doctrines. It has been only during comparatively short periods of transition, when public opinion was passing over from one political creed to another, that the decisions of the federal judiciary have been distinctly opposed to the principles of the ruling political party.

But, besides and above all this, the national courts are for the most part in the power of Congress. Even the Supreme Court is not beyond its control; for it is the legislative privilege to increase, whenever the legislative will so pleases, the number of the judges upon the supreme bench,—to "dilute the Constitution," as Webster once put it, "by creating a court which shall construe away its provisions"; and this on one memorable occasion it did choose to do. In December, 1869, the Supreme Court decided against the constitutionality of the Congress's pet Legal Tender Acts; and in the following March a vacancy on the bench opportunely occurring, and a new justiceship having been created to meet the emergency, the Senate gave the President to understand that no nominee unfavorable to the debated acts would be confirmed, two justices of the predominant party's way of thinking were appointed, the hostile majority of the court was outvoted, and the obnoxious decision reversed.[16]

The creation of additional justiceships is not, however, the only means by which Congress can coerce and control the Supreme Court. It may forestall an adverse decision by summarily depriving the court of jurisdiction over the case in which such a decision was threatened,[17] and that even while the case is pending; for only a very small part of the jurisdiction of even the Supreme Court is derived directly from the Constitution. Most of it is founded upon the Judiciary Act of 1789, which, being a mere act of Congress, may be repealed at any time that Congress chooses to repeal it. Upon this Judiciary Act, too, depend not only the powers but also the very existence of the inferior courts of the United States, the Circuit and District Courts; and their possible fate, in case of a conflict with Congress, is significantly foreshadowed in that Act of 1802 by which a democratic Congress swept away, root and branch, the system of circuit courts which had been created in the previous year, but which was hateful to the newly-successful Democrats because it had been officered with Federalists in the last hours of John Adams's administration.

This balance of judiciary against legislature and executive would seem, therefore, to be another of those ideal balances which are to be found in the books rather than in the rough realities of actual practice; for manifestly the power of the courts is safe only during seasons of political peace, when parties are not aroused to passion or tempted by the command of irresistible majorities.

As for some of the other constitutional balances enumerated in that passage of the letter to John Taylor which I have taken as a text, their present inefficacy is quite too plain to need proof. The constituencies may have been balanced against their representatives in Mr. Adams's day, for that was not a day of primaries and of strict caucus discipline. The legislatures of the States, too, may have been able to exercise some appreciable influence upon the action of the Senate, if those were days when policy was the predominant consideration which determined elections to the Senate, and the legislative choice was not always a matter of astute management, of mere personal weight, or party expediency; and the presidential electors undoubtedly did have at one time some freedom of choice in naming the chief magistrate, but before the third presidential election some of them were pledged, before Adams wrote this letter the majority of them were wont to obey the dictates of a congressional caucus, and for the last fifty years they have simply registered the will of party conventions.

It is noteworthy that Mr. Adams, possibly because he had himself been President, describes the executive as constituting only *"in some degree"* a check upon Congress, though he puts no such limitation upon the other balances of the system. Independently of experience, however, it might reasonably have been expected that the prerogatives of the President would have been one of the most effectual restraints upon the power of Congress. He was constituted one of the three great coördinate branches of the government; his functions were made of the highest dignity; his privileges many and substantial—so great, indeed, that it has pleased the fancy of some writers to parade them as exceeding those of the British crown; and there can be little doubt that, had the presidential chair always been filled by men of commanding character, of acknowledged ability, and of thorough political training, it would have continued to be a seat of the highest authority and consideration, the true centre of the federal structure, the real throne of administration, and the frequent source of policies. Washington and his Cabinet commanded the ear of Congress, and gave shape to its deliberations; Adams, though often crossed and thwarted, gave character to the government; and Jefferson, as President no less than as Secretary of State, was the real leader of his party. But the prestige of the presidential office has declined with the character of the Presidents. And the character of the Presidents has declined as the perfection of selfish party tactics has advanced.

It was inevitable that it should be so. After independence of choice on the part of the presidential electors had given place to the choice of presidential candidates by party conventions, it became absolutely necessary, in the eyes of politicans, and more and more necessary as time went on, to make expediency and availability the only rules of selection. As each party, when in convention assembled, spoke only those opinions which seemed to have received the sanction of the general voice, carefully suppressing in its "platform" all unpopular political tenets, and scrupulously omitting mention of every doctrine that might be looked upon as characteristic and as part of a peculiar and original programme, so, when the presidential candidate came to be chosen, it was recognized as imperatively necessary that he should have as short a political record as possible, and that he should wear a clean and irreproachable insignificance. "Gentlemen," said a distinguished American public man, "I would make an excellent President, but a very poor candidate." A decisive career which gives a man a well-understood place in public estimation constitutes a positive disability for the presidency; because candidacy must precede election, and the shoals of candidacy can be passed only by a light boat which carries little freight and can be turned readily about to suit the intricacies of the passage.

I am disposed to think, however, that the decline in the character of the Presidents is not the cause, but only the accompanying manifestation, of the declining prestige of the presidential office. That high office has fallen from its first estate of dignity because its power has waned; and its power has waned because the power of Congress has become predominant. The early Presidents were, as I have said, men of such a stamp that they would under any circumstances have made their influence felt; but their opportunities were exceptional. What with quarreling and fighting with England, buying Louisiana and Florida, building dykes to keep out the flood of the French Revolution, and extricating the country from ceaseless broils with the South American Republics, the government was, as has been pointed out, constantly busy, during the first quarter century of its existence, with the adjustment of foreign relations; and with foreign relations, of course, the Presidents had everything to do, since theirs was the office of negotiation.

Moreover, as regards home policy also those times were not like ours. Congress was somewhat awkward in exercising its untried powers, and its machinery was new, and without that fine adjustment which has since made it perfect of its kind.

Not having as yet learned the art of governing itself to the best advantage, and being without that facility of legislation which it afterwards acquired, the Legislature was glad to get guidance and suggestions of policy from the Executive.

But this state of things did not last long. Congress was very quick and apt in learning what it could do and in getting into thoroughly good trim to do it. It very early divided itself into standing committees which it equipped with very comprehensive and thorough-going privileges of legislative initiative and control, and set itself through these to administer the government. Congress is (to adopt Mr. Bagehot's description of Parliament) "nothing less than a big meeting of more or less idle people. In proportion as you give it power it will inquire into everything, settle everything, meddle in everything. In an ordinary despotism the powers of the despot are limited by his bodily capacity, and by the calls of pleasure; he is but one man; there are but twelve hours in his day, and he is not disposed to employ more than a small part in dull business: he keeps the rest for the court, or the harem, or for society." But Congress "is a despot who has unlimited time,—who has unlimited vanity,—who has, or believes he has, unlimited comprehension,—whose pleasure is in action, whose life is work." Accordingly it has entered more and more into the details of administration, until it has virtually taken into its own hands all the substantial powers of government. It does not domineer over the President himself, but it makes the Secretaries its humble servants. Not that it would hesitate, upon occasion, to deal directly with the chief magistrate himself; but it has few calls to do so, because our latter-day Presidents live by proxy; they are the executive in theory, but the Secretaries are the executive in fact. At the very first session of Congress steps were taken towards parceling out executive work amongst several departments, according to a then sufficiently thorough division of labor; and if the President of that day was not able to direct administrative details, of course the President of today is infinitely less able to do so, and must content himself with such general supervision as he may find time to exercise. He is in all every-day concerns shielded by the responsibility of his subordinates.

It cannot be said that this change has raised the cabinet in dignity or power; it has only altered their relations to the scheme of government. The members of the President's cabinet have always been prominent in administration; and certainly the early cabinets were no less strong in political influence than are the cabinets of our own day; but they were then only the President's advisers, whereas they are now rather the President's colleagues. The President is now scarcely the executive; he is the head of the administration; he appoints the executive. Of course this is not a legal principle; it is only a fact. In legal theory the President can control every operation of every department of the executive branch of the government; but in fact it is not practicable for him to do so, and a limitation of fact is as potent as a prohibition of law.

But, though the heads of the executive departments are thus no longer simply the counselors of the President, having become in a very real sense members of the executive, their guiding power in the conduct of affairs, instead of advancing, has steadily diminished; because while they were being made integral parts of the machinery of administration, Congress was extending its own sphere of activity, was getting into the habit of investigating and managing everything. The executive was losing and Congress gaining weight; and the station to which cabinets finally attained was a station of diminished and diminishing power. There is no distincter tendency in congressional history than the tendency to subject even the details of administration to the constant supervision, and all policy to the watchful intervention, of the Standing Committees.

I am inclined to think, therefore, that the enlarged powers of Congress are the fruits rather of an immensely increased efficiency of organization, and of the redoubled activity consequent upon the facility of action secured by such organization, than of any definite and persistent scheme of conscious usurpation. It is safe to say that Congress always had the desire to have a hand in every affair of federal government; but it was only by degrees that it found means and opportunity to gratify that desire, and its activity, extending its bounds wherever perfected processes of congressional work offered favoring prospects, has been enlarged so naturally and so silently that it has almost always seemed of normal extent, and has never, except perhaps during one or two brief periods of extraordinary political disturbance, appeared to reach much beyond its acknowledged constitutional sphere.

It is only in the exercise of those functions of public and formal consultation and coöperation with the President which are the peculiar offices of the Senate, that the power of Congress has made itself offensive to popular conceptions of constitutional propriety, because it is only in the exercise of such functions that Congress is compelled to be overt and demonstrative in its claims of over-lordship. The House of Representatives has made very few noisy demonstrations of its usurped right of ascendency; not because it was diffident or unambitious, but because it could maintain and extend its prerogatives quite as satisfactorily without noise; whereas the aggressive policy of the Senate has, in the acts of its "executive sessions," necessarily been overt, in spite of the closing of the doors, because when acting as the President's council in the ratification of treaties and in appointments to office its competition for power has been more formally and directly a contest with the executive than were those really more significant legislative acts by which, in conjunction with the House, it has habitually forced the heads of the executive departments to observe the will of Congress at every important turn of policy. Hence it is that to the superficial view it appears that only the Senate has been outrageous in its encroachments upon executive privilege. It is not often easy to see the true constitutional bearing of strictly legislative action; but it is patent even to the least observant that in the matter of appointments to office, for instance, senators have often outrun their legal right to give or withhold their assent to appointments, by insisting upon being first consulted concerning nominations as well, and have thus made their constitutional assent to appointments dependent upon an unconstitutional control of nominations.

This particular usurpation has been put upon a very solid basis of law by that Tenure-of-Office Act, which took away from President Johnson, in an hour of party heat and passion, that independent power of removal from office with which the Constitution had invested him, but which he had used in a way that exasperated a Senate not of his own way of thinking. But though this teasing power of the Senate's in the matter of the federal patronage is repugnant enough to the original theory of the Constitution, it is likely to be quite nullified by that policy of civil-service reform which has gained so firm, and mayhap so lasting, a footing in our national legislation; and in no event would the control of the patronage by the Senate have unbalanced the federal system more seriously than it may some day be unbalanced by an irresponsible exertion of that body's semi-executive powers in regard to the foreign policy of the government. More than one passage in the history of our foreign relations illustrates the danger. During the simple congressional session of 1868-9, for example, the treaty-*marring* power of the Senate was exerted in a way that made the comparative weakness of the executive very conspicuous, and was ominous of very serious results. It showed the executive in the right, but feeble and irresolute; the Senate masterful, though in the wrong. Denmark had been asked to part with the island of St. Thomas to the United States, and had at first refused all terms, not only because she cared little for the price, but also and principally because such a sale as that proposed was opposed to the established policy of the powers of Western Europe, in whose favor Denmark wished to stand; but finally, by stress of persistent and importunate negotiation, she had been induced to yield; a treaty had been signed and sent to the Senate; the people of St. Thomas had signified their consent to the cession by a formal vote; and the island had been actually transferred to an authorized agent of our government, upon the faith, on the part of the Danish ministers, that our representatives would not have trifled with them by entering upon an important business transaction which they were not assured of their ability to conclude. But the Senate let the treaty lie neglected in its committee-room; the limit of time agreed upon for confirmation passed; the Danish government, at last bent upon escaping the ridiculous humiliation that would follow a failure of the business at that stage, extended the time and even sent over one of its most eminent ministers of state to urge the negotiation by all dignified means; but the Senate cared nothing for Danish feelings and could afford, it thought, to despise President Grant and Mr. Fish, and at the next session rejected the treaty, and left the Danes to repossess themselves of the island, which we had concluded not to buy after all.

It was during this same session of 1868-9 that the Senate teased the executive by throwing every possible obstacle in the way of the confirmation of the much more important treaty with Great Britain relative to the Alabama claims, nearly marring for good and all one of the most satisfactory successes of our recent foreign policy;[18] but it is not necessary to dwell at length upon these well-known incidents of our later history, inasmuch as these are only two of innumerable instances which make it safe to say that from whatever point we view the relations of the executive and the legislature, it is evident that the power of the latter has steadily increased at the expense of the prerogatives of the former, and that the degree in which the one of these great branches of government is balanced against the other is a very insignificant degree indeed. For in the exercise of his power of veto, which is of course, beyond all comparison, his most formidable prerogative, the President acts not as the executive but as a third branch of the legislature. As Oliver Ellsworth said, at the first session of the Senate, the President is, as regards the passage of bills, but a part of Congress; and he can be an efficient, imperative member of the legislative system only in quiet times, when parties are pretty evenly balanced, and there are no indomitable majorities to tread obnoxious vetoes under foot.

Even this rapid outline sketch of the two pictures, of the theory and of the actual practices of the Constitution, has been sufficient, therefore, to show the most marked points of difference between the two, and to justify that careful study of congressional government, as the real government of the Union, which I am about to undertake. The balances of the Constitution are for the most part only ideal. For all practical purposes the national government is supreme over the state governments, and Congress predominant over its so-called coördinate branches. Whereas Congress at first overshadowed neither President nor federal judiciary, it now on occasion rules both with easy mastery and with a high hand; and whereas each State once guarded its sovereign prerogatives with jealous pride, and able men not a few preferred political advancement under the governments of the great commonwealths to office under the new federal Constitution, seats in state legislatures are now no longer coveted except as possible approaches to seats in Congress; and even governors of States seek election to the national Senate as a promotion, a reward for the humbler services they have rendered their local governments.

What makes it the more important to understand the present mechanism of national government, and to study the methods of congressional rule in a light unclouded by theory, is that there is plain evidence that the expansion of federal power is to continue, and that there exists, consequently, an evident necessity that it should be known just what to do and how to do it, when the time comes for public opinion to take control of the forces which are changing the character of our Constitution. There are voices in the air which cannot be misunderstood. The times seem to favor a centralization of governmental functions such as could not have suggested itself as a possibility to the framers of the Constitution. Since they gave their work to the world the whole face of that world has changed. The Constitution was adopted when it was six days' hard traveling from New York to Boston; when to cross East River was to venture a perilous voyage; when men were thankful for weekly mails; when the extent of the country's commerce was reckoned not in millions but in thousands of dollars; when the country knew few cities, and had but begun manufactures; when Indians were pressing upon near frontiers; when there were no telegraph lines, and no monster corporations. Unquestionably, the pressing problems of the present moment regard the regulation of our vast systems of commerce and manufacture, the control of giant corporations, the restraint of monopolies, the perfection of fiscal arrangements, the facilitating of economic exchanges, and many other like national concerns, amongst which may possibly be numbered the question of marriage and divorce; and the greatest of these problems do not fall within even the enlarged sphere of the federal government; some of them can be embraced within its jurisdiction by no possible stretch of construction, and the majority of them only by wresting the Constitution to strange and as yet unimagined uses. Still there is a distinct movement in favor of national control of all questions of policy which manifestly demand uniformity of treatment and power of administration such as cannot be realized by the separate, unconcerted action of the States; and it seems probable to many that, whether by constitutional amendment, or by still further flights of construction, yet broader territory will at no very distant day be assigned to the federal government. It becomes a matter of the utmost importance, therefore, both for those who would arrest this tendency, and for those who, because they look upon it with allowance if not with positive favor, would let it run its course, to examine critically the government upon which this new weight of responsibility and power seems likely to be cast, in order that its capacity both for the work it now does and for that which it may be called upon to do may be definitely estimated.

Judge Cooley, in his admirable work on "The Principles of American Constitutional Law," after quoting Mr. Adams's enumeration of the checks and balances of the federal system, adds this comment upon Mr. Adams's concluding statement that that system is an invention of our own. "The invention, nevertheless, was suggested by the British Constitution, in which a system almost equally elaborate was then in force. In its outward forms that system still remains; but there has been for more than a century a gradual change in the direction of a concentration of legislative and executive power in the popular house of Parliament, so that the government now is sometimes said, with no great departure from the fact, to be a government by the House of Commons." But Judge Cooley does not seem to see, or, if he sees, does not emphasize the fact, that our own system has been hardly less subject to "a gradual change in the direction of a concentration" of all the substantial powers of government in the hands of Congress; so that it is now, though a wide departure from the form of things, "no great departure from the fact" to describe ours as a government by the Standing Committees of Congress. This fact is, however, deducible from very many passages of Judge Cooley's own writings; for he is by no means insensible of that expansion of the powers of the federal government and that crystallization of its methods which have practically made obsolete the early constitutional theories, and even the modified theory which he himself seems to hold.

He has tested the nice adjustment of the theoretical balances by the actual facts, and has carefully set forth the results; but he has nowhere brought those results together into a single comprehensive view which might serve as a clear and satisfactory delineation of the Constitution of to-day; nor has he, or any other writer of capacity, examined minutely and at length that internal organization of Congress which determines its methods of legislation, which shapes its means of governing the executive departments, which contains in it the whole mechanism whereby the policy of the country is in all points directed, and which is therefore an essential branch of constitutional study. As the House of Commons is the central object of examination in every study of the English Constitution, so should Congress be in every study of our own. Any one who is unfamiliar with what Congress actually does and how it does it, with all its duties and all its occupations, with all its devices of management and resources of power, is very far from a knowledge of the constitutional system under which we live; and to every one who knows these things that knowledge is very near.

TWO

No more vital truth was ever uttered than that freedom and free institutions cannot long be maintained by any people who do not understand the nature of their own government.

THE HOUSE OF REPRESENTATIVES

Like a vast picture thronged with figures of equal prominence and crowded with elaborate and obtrusive details, Congress is hard to see satisfactorily and appreciatively at a single view and from a single stand-point. Its complicated forms and diversified structure confuse the vision, and conceal the system which underlies its composition. It is too complex to be understood without an effort, without a careful and systematic process of analysis. Consequently, very few people do understand it, and its doors are practically shut against the comprehension of the public at large. If Congress had a few authoritative leaders whose figures were very distinct and very conspicuous to the eye of the world, and who could represent and stand for the national legislature in the thoughts of that very numerous, and withal very respectable, class of persons who must think specifically and in concrete forms when they think at all, those persons who can make something out of men but very little out of intangible generalizations, it would be quite within the region of possibilities for the majority of the nation to follow the course of legislation without any very serious confusion of thought. I suppose that almost everybody who just now gives any heed to the policy of Great Britain, with regard even to the reform of the franchise and other like strictly legislative questions, thinks of Mr. Gladstone and his colleagues rather than of the House of Commons, whose servants they are. The question is not, What will Parliament do? but, What will Mr. Gladstone do? And there is even less doubt that it is easier and more natural to look upon the legislative designs of Germany as locked up behind Bismarck's heavy brows than to think of them as dependent upon the determinations of the Reichstag, although as a matter of fact its consent is indispensable even to the plans of the imperious and domineering Chancellor.

But there is no great minister or ministry to represent the will and being of Congress in the common thought. The Speaker of the House of Representatives stands as near to leadership as any one; but his will does not run as a formative and imperative power in legislation much beyond the appointment of the committees who are to lead the House and do its work for it, and it is, therefore, not entirely satisfactory to the public mind to trace all legislation to him. He may have a controlling hand in starting it; but he sits too still in his chair, and is too evidently not on the floor of the body over which he presides, to make it seem probable to the ordinary judgment that he has much immediate concern in legislation after it is once set afoot. Everybody knows that he is a staunch and avowed partisan, and that he likes to make smooth, whenever he can, the legislative paths of his party; but it does not seem likely that all important measures originate with him, or that he is the author of every distinct policy. And in fact he is not. He is a great party chief, but the hedging circumstances of his official position as presiding officer prevent his performing the part of active leadership. He appoints the leaders of the House, but he is not himself its leader.

The leaders of the House are the chairmen of the principal Standing Committees. Indeed, to be exactly accurate, the House has as many leaders as there are subjects of legislation; for there are as many Standing Committees as there are leading classes of legislation, and in the consideration of every topic of business the House is guided by a special leader in the person of the chairman of the Standing Committee, charged with the superintendence of measures of the particular class to which that topic belongs. It is this multiplicity of leaders, this many-headed leadership, which makes the organization of the House too complex to afford uninformed people and unskilled observers any easy clue to its methods of rule. For the chairmen of the Standing Committees do not constitute a coöperative body like a ministry. They do not consult and concur in the adoption of homogeneous and mutually helpful measures; there is no thought of acting in concert. Each Committee goes its own way at its own pace. It is impossible to discover any unity or method in the disconnected and therefore unsystematic, confused, and desultory action of the House, or any common purpose in the measures which its Committees from time to time recommend.

And it is not only to the unanalytic thought of the common observer who looks at the House from the outside that its doings seem helter-skelter, and without comprehensible rule; it is not at once easy to understand them when they are scrutinized in their daily headway through open session by one who is inside the House. The newly-elected member, entering its doors for the first time, and with no more knowledge of its rules and customs than the more intelligent of his constituents possess, always experiences great difficulty in adjusting his preconceived ideas of congressional life to the strange and unlooked-for conditions by which he finds himself surrounded after he has been sworn in and has become a part of the great legislative machine. Indeed there are generally many things connected with his career in Washington to disgust and dispirit, if not to aggrieve, the new member. In the first place, his local reputation does not follow him to the federal capital. Possibly the members from his own State know him, and receive him into full fellowship; but no one else knows him, except as an adherent of this or that party, or as a new-comer from this or that State. He finds his station insignificant, and his identity indistinct. But this social humiliation which he experiences in circles in which to be a congressman does not of itself confer distinction, because it is only to be one among many, is probably not to be compared with the chagrin and disappointment which come in company with the inevitable discovery that he is equally without weight or title to consideration in the House itself. No man, when chosen to the membership of a body possessing great powers and exalted prerogatives, likes to find his activity repressed, and himself suppressed, by imperative rules and precedents which seem to have been framed for the deliberate purpose of making usefulness unattainable by individual members. Yet such the new member finds the rules and precedents of the House to be. It matters not to him, because it is not apparent on the face of things, that those rules and precedents have grown, not out of set purpose to curtail the privileges of new members as such, but out of the plain necessities of business; it remains the fact that he suffers under their curb, and it is not until "custom hath made it in him a property of easiness" that he submits to them with anything like good grace.

Not all new members suffer alike, of course, under this trying discipline; because it is not every new member that comes to his seat with serious purposes of honest, earnest, and duteous work. There are numerous tricks and subterfuges, soon learned and easily used, by means of which the most idle and self-indulgent members may readily make such show of exemplary diligence as will quite satisfy, if it does not positively delight, constituents in Buncombe. But the number of congressmen who deliberately court uselessness and counterfeit well-doing is probably small. The great majority doubtless have a keen enough sense of their duty, and a sufficiently unhesitating desire to do it; and it may safely be taken for granted that the zeal of new members is generally hot and insistent. If it be not hot to begin with, it is like to become so by reason of friction with the rules, because such men must inevitably be chafed by the bonds of restraint drawn about them by the inexorable observances of the House.

Often the new member goes to Washington as the representative of a particular line of policy, having been elected, it may be, as an advocate of free trade, or as a champion of protection; and it is naturally his first care upon entering on his duties to seek immediate opportunity for the expression of his views and immediate means of giving them definite shape and thrusting them upon the attention of Congress. His disappointment is, therefore, very keen when he finds both opportunity and means denied him. He can introduce his bill; but that is all he can do, and he must do that at a particular time and in a particular manner. This he is likely to learn through rude experience, if he be not cautious to inquire beforehand the details of practice. He is likely to make a rash start, upon the supposition that Congress observes the ordinary rules of parliamentary practice to which he has become accustomed in the debating clubs familiar to his youth, and in the mass-meetings known to his later experience. His bill is doubtless ready for presentation early in the session, and some day, taking advantage of a pause in the proceedings, when there seems to be no business before the House, he rises to read it and move its adoption. But he finds getting the floor an arduous and precarious undertaking. There are certain to be others who want it as well as he; and his indignation is stirred by the fact that the Speaker does not so much as turn towards him, though he must have heard his call, but recognizes some one else readily and as a matter of course. If he be obstreperous and persistent in his cries of "Mr. Speaker," he may get that great functionary's attention for a moment,—only to be told, however, that he is out of order, and that his bill can be introduced at that stage only by unanimous consent: immediately there are mechanically-uttered but emphatic exclamations of objection, and he is forced to sit down confused and disgusted. He has, without knowing it, obtruded himself in the way of the "regular order of business," and been run over in consequence, without being quite clear as to how the accident occurred.

Moved by the pain and discomfiture of this first experience to respect, if not to fear, the rules, the new member casts about, by study or inquiry, to find out, if possible, the nature and occasion of his privileges. He learns that his only safe day is Monday. On that day the roll of the States is called, and members may introduce bills as their States are reached in the call. So on Monday he essays another bout with the rules, confident this time of being on their safe side,—but mayhap indiscreetly and unluckily over-confident. For if he supposes, as he naturally will, that after his bill has been sent up to be read by the clerk he may say a few words in its behalf, and in that belief sets out upon his long-considered remarks, he will be knocked down by the rules as surely as he was on the first occasion when he gained the floor for a brief moment. The rap of Mr. Speaker's gavel is sharp, immediate, and peremptory. He is curtly informed that no debate is in order; the bill can only be referred to the appropriate Committee.

This is, indeed, disheartening; it is his first lesson in committee government, and the master's rod smarts; but the sooner he learns the prerogatives and powers of the Standing Committees the sooner will he penetrate the mysteries of the rules and avoid the pain of further contact with their thorny side. The privileges of the Standing Committees are the beginning and the end of the rules. Both the House of Representatives and the Senate conduct their business by what may figuratively, but not inaccurately, be called an odd device of *disintegration*. The House virtually both deliberates and legislates in small sections. Time would fail it to discuss all the bills brought in, for they every session number thousands; and it is to be doubted whether, even if time allowed, the ordinary processes of debate and amendment would suffice to sift the chaff from the wheat in the bushels of bills every week piled upon the clerk's desk. Accordingly, no futile attempt is made to do anything of the kind. The work is parceled out, most of it to the forty-seven Standing Committees which constitute the regular organization of the House, some of it to select committees appointed for special and temporary purposes. Each of the almost numberless bills that come pouring in on Mondays is "read a first and second time,"—simply perfunctorily read, that is, by its title, by the clerk, and passed by silent assent through its first formal courses, for the purpose of bringing it to the proper stage for commitment,—and referred without debate to the appropriate Standing Committee. Practically, no bill escapes commitment—save, of course, bills introduced by committees, and a few which may now and then be crowded through under a suspension of the rules, granted by a two-thirds vote—though the exact disposition to be made of a bill is not always determined easily and as a matter of course. Besides the great Committee of Ways and Means and the equally great Committee on Appropriations, there are Standing Committees on Banking and Currency, on Claims, on Commerce, on the Public Lands, on Post-Offices and Post-Roads, on the Judiciary, on Public Expenditures, on Manufactures, on Agriculture, on Military Affairs, on Naval Affairs, on Mines and Mining, on Education and Labor, on Patents, and on a score of other branches of legislative concern; but careful and differential as is the topical division of the subjects of legislation which is represented in the titles of these Committees, it is not always evident to which Committee each particular bill should go. Many bills affect subjects which may be regarded as lying as properly within the jurisdiction of one as of another of the Committees; for no hard and fast lines separate the various classes of business which the Committees are commissioned to take in charge. Their jurisdictions overlap at many points, and it must frequently happen that bills are read which cover just this common ground. Over the commitment of such bills sharp and interesting skirmishes often take place. There is active competition for them, the ordinary, quiet routine of matter-of-course reference being interrupted by rival motions seeking to give very different directions to the disposition to be made of them. To which Committee should a bill "to fix and establish the maximum rates of fares of the Union Pacific and Central Pacific Railroads" be sent,—to the Committee on Commerce or to the Committee on the Pacific Railroads? Should a bill which prohibits the mailing of certain classes of letters and circulars go to the Committee on Post-Offices and Post-Roads, because it relates to the mails, or to the Committee on the Judiciary, because it proposes to make any transgression of its prohibition a crime? What is the proper disposition of any bill which thus seems to lie within two distinct committee jurisdictions?

The fate of bills committed is generally not uncertain. As a rule, a bill committed is a bill doomed. When it goes from the clerk's desk to a committee-room it crosses a parliamentary bridge of sighs to dim dungeons of silence whence it will never return. The means and time of its death are unknown, but its friends never see it again. Of course no Standing Committee is privileged to take upon itself the full powers of the House it represents, and formally and decisively reject a bill referred to it; its disapproval, if it disapproves, must be reported to the House in the form of a recommendation that the bill "do not pass." But it is easy, and therefore common, to let the session pass without making any report at all upon bills deemed objectionable or unimportant, and to substitute for reports upon them a few bills of the Committee's own drafting; so that thousands of bills expire with the expiration of each Congress, not having been rejected, but having been simply neglected. There was not time to report upon them.

Of course it goes without saying that the practical effect of this Committee organization of the House is to consign to each of the Standing Committees the entire direction of legislation upon those subjects which properly come to its consideration. As to those subjects it is entitled to the initiative, and all legislative action with regard to them is under its overruling guidance. It gives shape and course to the determinations of the House. In one respect, however, its initiative is limited. Even a Standing Committee cannot report a bill whose subject-matter has not been referred to it by the House, "by the rules or otherwise"; it cannot volunteer advice on questions upon which its advice has not been asked. But this is not a serious, not even an operative, limitation upon its functions of suggestion and leadership; for it is a very simple matter to get referred to it any subject it wishes to introduce to the attention of the House. Its chairman, or one of its leading members, frames a bill covering the point upon which the Committee wishes to suggest legislation; brings it in, in his capacity as a private member, on Monday, when the call of States is made; has it referred to his Committee; and thus secures an opportunity for the making of the desired report.

It is by this imperious authority of the Standing Committees that the new member is stayed and thwarted whenever he seeks to take an active part in the business of the House. Turn which way he may, some privilege of the Committees stands in his path. The rules are so framed as to put all business under their management; and one of the discoveries which the new member is sure to make, albeit after many trying experiences and sobering adventures and as his first session draws towards its close, is, that under their sway freedom of debate finds no place of allowance, and that his long-delayed speech must remain unspoken. For even a long congressional session is too short to afford time for a full consideration of all the reports of the forty-seven Committees, and debate upon them must be rigidly cut short, if not altogether excluded, if any considerable part of the necessary business is to be gotten through with before adjournment. There are some subjects to which the House must always give prompt attention; therefore reports from the Committees on Printing and on Elections are always in order; and there are some subjects to which careful consideration must always be accorded; therefore the Committee of Ways and Means and the Committee on Appropriations are clothed with extraordinary privileges; and revenue and supply bills may be reported, and will ordinarily be considered, at any time. But these four are the only specially licensed Committees. The rest must take their turns in fixed order as they are called on by the Speaker, contenting themselves with such crumbs of time as fall from the tables of the four Committees of highest prerogative.

Senator Hoar, of Massachusetts, whose long congressional experience entitles him to speak with authority, calculates[1] that, "supposing the two sessions which make up the life of the House to last ten months," most of the Committees have at their disposal during each Congress but two hours apiece in which "to report upon, debate, and dispose of all the subjects of general legislation committed to their charge." For of course much time is wasted. No Congress gets immediately to work upon its first assembling. It has its officers to elect, and after their election some time must elapse before its organization is finally completed by the appointment of the Committees. It adjourns for holidays, too, and generally spares itself long sittings. Besides, there are many things to interrupt the call of the Committees upon which most of the business waits. That call can proceed only during the morning hours, —the hours just after the reading of the "Journal,"—on Tuesdays, Wednesdays, and Thursdays; and even then it may suffer postponement because of the unfinished business of the previous day which is entitled to first consideration. The call cannot proceed on Mondays because the morning hour of Mondays is devoted invariably to the call of the States for the introduction of bills and resolutions; nor on Fridays, for Friday is "private bill day," and is always engrossed by the Committee on Claims, or by other fathers of bills which have gone upon the "private calendar." On Saturdays the House seldom sits.

The reports made during these scant morning hours are ordered to be printed, for future consideration in their turn, and the bills introduced by the Committees are assigned to the proper calendars, to be taken up in order at the proper time. When a morning hour has run out, the House hastens to proceed with the business on the Speaker's table.

These are some of the plainer points of the rules. They are full of complexity, and of confusion to the uninitiated, and the confusions of practice are greater than the confusions of the rules. For the regular order of business is constantly being interrupted by the introduction of resolutions offered "by unanimous consent," and of bills let in under a "suspension of the rules." Still, it is evident that there is one principle which runs through every stage of procedure, and which is never disallowed or abrogated,—the principle that the Committees shall rule without let or hindrance. And this is a principle of extraordinary formative power. It is the mould of all legislation. In the first place, the speeding of business under the direction of the Committees determines the character and the amount of the discussion to which legislation shall be subjected. The House is conscious that time presses. It knows that, hurry as it may, it will hardly get through with one eighth of the business laid out for the session, and that to pause for lengthy debate is to allow the arrears to accumulate. Besides, most of the members are individually anxious to expedite action on every pending measure, because each member of the House is a member of one or more of the Standing Committees, and is quite naturally desirous that the bills prepared by his Committees, and in which he is, of course, specially interested by reason of the particular attention which he has been compelled to give them, should reach a hearing and a vote as soon as possible. It must, therefore, invariably happen that the Committee holding the floor at any particular time is the Committee whose proposals the majority wish to dispose of as summarily as circumstances will allow, in order that the rest of the forty-two unprivileged Committees to which the majority belong may gain the earlier and the fairer chance of a hearing. A reporting Committee, besides, is generally as glad to be pushed as the majority are to push it. It probably has several bills matured, and wishes to see them disposed of before its brief hours of opportunity[2] are passed and gone.

Consequently, it is the established custom of the House to accord the floor for one hour to the member of the reporting Committee who has charge of the business under consideration; and that hour is made the chief hour of debate. The reporting committee-man seldom, if ever, uses the whole of the hour himself for his opening remarks; he uses part of it, and retains control of the rest of it; for by undisputed privilege it is his to dispose of, whether he himself be upon the floor or not. No amendment is in order during that hour, unless he consent to its presentation; and he does not, of course, yield his time indiscriminately to any one who wishes to speak. He gives way, indeed, as in fairness he should, to opponents as well as to friends of the measure under his charge; but generally no one is accorded a share of his time who has not obtained his previous promise of the floor; and those who do speak must not run beyond the number of minutes he has agreed to allow them. He keeps the course both of debate and of amendment thus carefully under his own supervision, as a good tactician, and before he finally yields the floor, at the expiration of his hour, he is sure to move the previous question. To neglect to do so would be to lose all control of the business in hand; for unless the previous question is ordered the debate may run on at will, and his Committee's chance for getting its measures through slip quite away; and that would be nothing less than his disgrace. He would be all the more blameworthy because he had but to ask for the previous question to get it. As I have said, the House is as eager to hurry business as he can be, and will consent to almost any

limitation of discussion that he may demand; though, probably, if he were to throw the reins upon its neck, it would run
at large from very wantonness, in scorn of such a driver. The
previous question once ordered, all amendments are precluded,
and one hour remains for the summing-up of this same privileged committee-man before the final vote is taken and the bill
disposed of.

These are the customs which baffle and perplex and astound
the new member. In these precedents and usages, when at
length he comes to understand them, the novice spies out the
explanation of the fact, once so confounding and seemingly
inexplicable, that when he leaped to his feet to claim the floor
other members who rose after him were coolly and unfeel-
ingly preferred before him by the Speaker. Of course it is
plain enough now that Mr. Speaker knew beforehand to whom
the representative of the reporting Committee had agreed to
yield the floor; and it was no use for any one else to cry out
for recognition. Whoever wished to speak should, if possible,
have made some arrangement with the Committee before the
business came to a hearing, and should have taken care to
notify Mr. Speaker that he was to be granted the floor for a
few moments.

Unquestionably this, besides being a very interesting, is a
very novel and significant method of restricting debate and
expediting legislative action,—a method of very serious import, and obviously fraught with far-reaching constitutional
effects. The practices of debate which prevail in its legislative
assembly are manifestly of the utmost importance to a self-
governing people; for that legislation which is not thoroughly
discussed by the legislating body is practically done in a
corner. It is impossible for Congress itself to do wisely what
it does so hurriedly; and the constituencies cannot understand
what Congress does not itself stop to consider. The prerogatives of the Committees represent something more than a
mere convenient division of labor. There is only one part of
its business to which Congress, as a whole, attends,—that
part, namely, which is embraced under the privileged subjects
of revenue and supply. The House never accepts the proposals
of the Committee of Ways and Means, or of the Committee

on Appropriations, without due deliberation; but it allows
almost all of its other Standing Committees virtually to legislate for it. In form, the Committees only digest the various
matter introduced by individual members, and prepare it,
with care, and after thorough investigation, for the final consideration and action of the House; but, in reality, they dictate
the course to be taken, prescribing the decisions of the House
not only, but measuring out, according to their own wills, its
opportunities for debate and deliberation as well. The House
sits, not for serious discussion, but to sanction the conclusions
of its Committees as rapidly as possible. It legislates in its
committee-rooms; not by the determinations of majorities,
but by the resolutions of specially-commissioned minorities;
so that it is not far from the truth to say that Congress in
session is Congress on public exhibition, whilst Congress in
its committee-rooms is Congress at work.

Habit grows fast, even upon the unconventional American,
and the nature of the House of Representatives has, by long
custom, been shaped to the spirit of its rules. Representatives
have attained, by rigorous self-discipline, to the perfect stature
of the law under which they live, having purged their hearts
as completely as may be of all desire to do that which it is the
chief object of that law to forbid by giving over a vain lust
after public discussion. The entire absence of the instinct of
debate amongst them, and their apparent unfamiliarity with
the idea of combating a proposition by argument, was recently
illustrated by an incident which was quite painfully amusing.
The democratic majority of the House of the Forty-eighth
Congress desired the immediate passage of a pension bill of
rather portentous proportions; but the republican minority
disapproved of the bill with great fervor, and, when it was
moved by the Pension Committee, late one afternoon, in a
thin House, that the rules be suspended, and an early day set
for a consideration of the bill, the Republicans addressed
themselves to determined and persistent "filibustering" to prevent action. First they refused to vote, leaving the Democrats
without an acting quorum; then, all night long, they kept the
House at roll-calling on dilatory and obstructive motions, the
dreary dragging of the time being relieved occasionally by

the amusement of hearing the excuses of members who had tried to slip off to bed, or by the excitement of an angry dispute between the leaders of the two parties as to the responsibility for the dead-lock. Not till the return of morning brought in the delinquents to recruit the democratic ranks did business advance a single step. Now, the noteworthy fact about this remarkable scene is, that the minority were not manœuvring to gain opportunity or time for debate, in order that the country might be informed of the true nature of the obnoxious bill, but were simply fighting a preliminary motion with silent, dogged obstruction. After the whole night had been spent in standing out against action, the House is said to have been "in no mood for the thirty-minutes' debate allowed by the rules," and a final vote was taken, with only a word or two said. It was easier and more natural, as everybody saw, to direct attention to the questionable character of what was being attempted by the majority by creating a somewhat scandalous "scene," of which every one would talk, than by making speeches which nobody would read. It was a notable commentary on the characteristic methods of our system of congressional government.

One very noteworthy result of this system is to shift the theatre of debate upon legislation from the floor of Congress to the privacy of the committee-rooms. Provincial gentlemen who read the Associated Press dispatches in their morning papers as they sit over their coffee at breakfast are doubtless often very sorely puzzled by certain of the items which sometimes appear in the brief telegraphic notes from Washington. What can they make of this for instance: "The House Committee on Commerce to-day heard arguments from the congressional delegation from" such and such States "in advocacy of appropriations for river and harbor improvements which the members desire incorporated in the River and Harbor Appropriations Bill"? They probably do not understand that it would have been useless for members not of the Committee on Commerce to wait for any opportunity to make their suggestions on the floor of Congress, where the measure to which they wish to make additions would be under the authoritative control of the Committee, and where, consequently, they could gain a hearing only by the courteous sufferance of the committee-man in charge of the report. Whatever is to be done must be done by or through the Committee.

It would seem, therefore, that practically Congress, or at any rate the House of Representatives, delegates not only its legislative but also its deliberative functions to its Standing Committees. The little public debate that arises under the stringent and urgent rules of the House is formal rather than effective, and it is the discussions which take place in the Committees that give form to legislation. Undoubtedly these siftings of legislative questions by the Committees are of great value in enabling the House to obtain "undarkened counsel" and intelligent suggestions from authoritative sources. All sober, purposeful, business-like talk upon questions of public policy, whether it take place in Congress or only before the Committees of Congress, is of great value; and the controversies which spring up in the committee-rooms, both amongst the committee-men themselves and between those who appear before the Committees as advocates of special measures, cannot but contribute to add clearness and definite consistency to the reports submitted to the House.

There are, however, several very obvious reasons why the most thorough canvass of business by the Committees, and the most exhaustive and discriminating discussion of all its details in their rooms, cannot take the place or fulfill the uses of amendment and debate by Congress in open session. In the first place, the proceedings of the Committees are private and their discussions unpublished. The chief, and unquestionably the most essential, object of all discussion of public business is the enlightenment of public opinion; and of course, since it cannot hear the debates of the Committees, the nation is not apt to be much instructed by them. Only the Committees are enlightened. There is a conclusive objection to the publication of the proceedings of the Committees, which is recognized as of course by all parliamentary lawyers, namely, that those proceedings are of no force till confirmed by the House. A Committee is commissioned, not to instruct the public, but to instruct and guide the House.

Indeed it is not usual for the Committees to open their

sittings often to those who desire to be heard with regard to pending questions; and no one can demand a hearing as of right. On the contrary, they are privileged and accustomed to hold their sessions in absolute secrecy. It is made a breach of order for any member to allude on the floor of the House to anything that has taken place in committee, "unless by a written report sanctioned by a majority of the Committee"; and there is no place in the regular order of business for a motion instructing a Committee to conduct its investigations with open doors. Accordingly, it is only by the concession of the Committees that arguments are made before them.

When they do suffer themselves to be approached, moreover, they generally extend the leave to others besides their fellow-congressmen. The Committee on Commerce consents to listen to prominent railroad officials upon the subject of the regulation of freight charges and fares; and scores of interested persons telegraph inquiries to the chairman of the Committee of Ways and Means as to the time at which they are to be permitted to present to the Committee their views upon the revision of the tariff. The speeches made before the Committees at their open sessions are, therefore, scarcely of such a kind as would be instructive to the public, and on that account worth publishing. They are as a rule the pleas of special pleaders, the arguments of advocates. They have about them none of the searching, critical, illuminating character of the higher order of parliamentary debate, in which men are pitted against each other as equals, and urged to sharp contest and masterful strife by the inspiration of political principle and personal ambition, through the rivalry of parties and the competition of policies. They represent a joust between antagonistic interests, not a contest of principles. They could scarcely either inform or elevate public opinion, even if they were to obtain its heed.

For the instruction and elevation of public opinion, in regard to national affairs, there is needed something more than special pleas for special privileges. There is needed public discussion of a peculiar sort: a discussion by the sovereign legislative body itself, a discussion in which every feature of each mooted point of policy shall be distinctly brought out, and every argument of significance pushed to the farthest point of insistence, by recognized leaders in that body; and, above all, a discussion upon which something—something of interest or importance, some pressing question of administration or of law, the fate of a party or the success of a conspicuous politician—evidently depends. It is only a discussion of this sort that the public will heed; no other sort will impress it.

There could, therefore, be no more unwelcome revelation to one who has anything approaching a statesman-like appreciation of the essential conditions of intelligent self-government than just that which must inevitably be made to every one who candidly examines our congressional system; namely, that, under that system, such discussion is impossible. There are, to begin with, physical and *architectural* reasons why business-like debate of public affairs by the House of Representatives is out of the question. To those who visit the galleries of the representative chamber during a session of the House these reasons are as obvious as they are astonishing. It would be natural to expect that a body which meets ostensibly for consultation and deliberation should hold its sittings in a room small enough to admit of an easy interchange of views and a ready concert of action, where its members would be brought into close, sympathetic contact; and it is nothing less than astonishing to find it spread at large through the vast spaces of such a chamber as the hall of the House of Representatives, where there are no close ranks of coöperating parties, but each member has a roomy desk and an easy revolving chair; where broad aisles spread and stretch themselves; where ample, soft-carpeted areas lie about the spacious desks of the Speaker and clerks; where deep galleries reach back from the outer limits of the wide passages which lie beyond "the bar": an immense, capacious chamber, disposing its giant dimensions freely beneath the great level lacunar ceiling through whose glass panels the full light of day pours in. The most vivid impression the visitor gets in looking over that vast hall is the impression of space. A speaker must needs have a voice like O'Connell's, the practical visitor is apt to think, as he sits in the gallery, to fill even the silent spaces of that room; how much more to overcome the disorderly noises that buzz and rattle through it when the representatives are assembled,—a voice clear, sonorous, dominant, like the voice of a clarion. One who speaks there with the voice and lungs of the ordinary mortal must content himself with the audience of those members in his own immediate neighborhood, whose ears he rudely assails in vehement efforts to command the attention of those beyond them, and who, therefore, cannot choose but hear him.

It is of this magnitude of the hall of the representatives that those news telegrams are significant which speak of an interesting or witty speech in Congress as having drawn about the speaker listeners from all parts of the House. As one of our most noted wits would say, a member must needs take a Sabbath day's journey to get within easy hearing distance of a speaker who is addressing the House from the opposite side of the hall; for besides the space there are the noises intervening, the noises of loud talking and of the clapping of hands for the pages, making the task of the member who is speaking "very like trying to address the people in the omnibuses from the curbstone in front of the Astor House." [3]

But these physical limitations to debate, though serious and real, are amongst the least important, because they are amongst the least insuperable. If effective and business-like public discussions were considered indispensable by Congress, or even desirable, the present chamber could readily be divided into two halls: the one a commodious reading-room where the members might chat and write at ease as they now do in the House itself; and the other a smaller room suitable for debate and earnest business. This, in fact, has been several times proposed, but the House does not feel that there is any urgency about providing facilities for debate, because it sees no reason to desire an increase of speech-making, in view of the fact that, notwithstanding all the limitations now put upon discussion, its business moves much too slowly. The early Congresses had time to talk; Congresses of to-day have not. Before that wing of the Capitol was built in which the representative chamber now is, the House used to sit in the much smaller room, now empty save for the statuary to whose exhibition it is devoted; and there much speech-making went on from day to day; there Calhoun and Randolph and Webster and Clay won their reputations as statesmen and orators. So earnest and interesting were the debates of those days, indeed, that the principal speeches delivered in Congress seem to have been usually printed at length in the metropolitan journals.[4] But the number and length of the speeches was even then very much deplored; and so early as 1828 a writer in the "North American Review" condemns what he calls "the habit of congressional debating," with the air of one who speaks against some abuse which every one acknowledges to be a nuisance.[5] Eleven years later a contributor to the "Democratic Review" [6] declared that it had "been gravely charged upon" Mr. Samuel Cushman, then a member of the Twenty-fifth Congress from New Hampshire, "that he moves the previous question. Truly," continues the essayist, "he does, and for that very service, if he had never done anything else, he deserves a monument as a public benefactor. One man who can arrest a tedious, long-winded, factious, time-killing debate, is worth forty who can provoke or keep one up. It requires some moral courage, some spirit, and some tact also, to move the previous questions, and to move it, too, at precisely the right point of time."

This ardent and generous defense of Mr. Cushman against the odious accusation of moving the previous question would doubtless be exquisitely amusing to the chairman of one of the Standing Committees of the Forty-eighth Congress, to whom the previous question seems one of the commonest necessities of life. But, after all, he ought not to laugh at the ingenuous essayist, for that was not the heydey of the rules; they then simply served and did not tyrannize over the House. They did not then have the opportunity of empire afforded them by the scantiness of time which hurries the House, and the weight of business which oppresses it; and they were at a greater disadvantage in a room where oratory was possible than they are in a vast chamber where the orator's voice is drowned amidst the noises of disorderly inattention. Nowadays would-be debaters are easily thrust out of Congress and forced to resort to the printing-office; are compelled to content themselves with speaking from the pages of the "Record" instead of from their places in the House. Some people who live very far from Washington may imagine that the speeches which are spread at large in the columns of the "Congressional Record," or which their representative sends them in pamphlet form, were actually delivered in Congress; but every one else knows that they were not; that Congress is constantly granting leave to its members to insert in the official reports of the proceedings speeches which it never heard and does not care to hear, but which it is not averse from printing at the public expense, if it is desirable that constituents and the country at large should read them. It will not stand between a member and his constituents so long as it can indulge the one and satisfy the others without any inconvenience to itself or any serious drain upon the resources of the Treasury. The public printer does not object.

But there are other reasons still more organic than these why the debates of Congress cannot, under our present system, have that serious purpose of search into the merits of policies and that definite and determinate party—or, if you will, partisan—aim without which they can never be effective for the instruction of public opinion, or the cleansing of political action. The chief of these reasons, because the parent of all the rest, is that there are in Congress no authoritative leaders who are the recognized spokesmen of their parties. Power is nowhere concentrated; it is rather deliberately and of set policy scattered amongst many small chiefs. It is divided up, as it were, into forty-seven seigniories, in each of which a Standing Committee is the court-baron and its chairman lord-proprietor. These petty barons, some of them not a little powerful, but none of them within reach of the full powers of rule, may at will exercise an almost despotic sway within their own shires, and may sometimes threaten to convulse even the realm itself; but both their mutual jealousies and their brief and restricted opportunities forbid their combining, and each is very far from the office of common leader.

I know that to some this scheme of distributed power and disintegrated rule seems a very excellent device whereby we are enabled to escape a dangerous "one-man power" and an untoward concentration of functions; and it is very easy to see and appreciate the considerations which make this view of committee government so popular. It is based upon a very proper and salutary fear of *irresponsible* power; and those who most resolutely maintain it always fight from the position that all leadership in legislation is hard to restrain in proportion to its size and to the strength of its prerogatives, and that to divide it is to make it manageable. They aver, besides, that the less a man has to do—that is to say, the more he is confined to single departments and to definite details—the more intelligent and thorough will his work be. They like the Committees, therefore, just because they are many and weak, being quite willing to abide their being despotic within their narrow spheres.

It seems evident, however, when the question is looked at from another stand-point, that, as a matter of fact and experience, the more power is divided the more irresponsible it becomes. A mighty baron who can call half the country to arms is watched with greater jealousy, and, therefore, restrained with more vigilant care than is ever vouchsafed the feeble master of a single and solitary castle. The one cannot stir abroad upon an innocent pleasure jaunt without attracting the suspicious attention of the whole country-side; the other may vex and harry his entire neighborhood without fear of let or hindrance. It is ever the little foxes that spoil the grapes. At any rate, to turn back from illustration to the facts of the argument, it is plain enough that the petty character of the leadership of each Committee contributes towards making its despotism sure by making its duties uninteresting. The Senate almost always discusses its business with considerable thoroughness; and even the House, whether by common consent or by reason of such persistent "filibustering" on the part of the minority as compels the reporting Committee and the majority to grant time for talk, sometimes stops to debate committee reports at length; but nobody, except, perhaps, newspaper editors, finds these debates interesting reading.

Why is it that many intelligent and patriotic people throughout this country, from Virginia to California,—people who, beyond all question, love their State and the Union more than they love our cousin state over sea,—subscribe for the London papers in order to devour the parliamentary debates, and yet would never think of troubling themselves to make tedious progress through a single copy of the "Congressional Record"? Is it because they are captivated by the old-world dignity of royal England with its nobility and its court pageantry, or because of a vulgar desire to appear better versed than their neighbors in foreign affairs, and to affect familiarity with British statesmen? No; of course not. It is because the parliamentary debates are interesting and ours are not. In the British House of Commons the functions and privileges of our Standing Committees are all concentrated in the hands of the Ministry, who have, besides, some prerogatives of leadership which even our Committees do not possess, so that they carry all responsibility as well as great power, and all debate wears an intense personal and party interest. Every important discussion is an arraignment of the Ministry by the Opposition,—an arraignment of the majority by the minority; and every important vote is a party defeat and a party triumph. The whole conduct of the government turns upon what is said in the Commons, because the revelations of debate often change votes, and a Ministry loses hold upon power as it loses hold upon the confidence of the Commons. This great Standing Committee goes out whenever it crosses the will of the majority. It is, therefore, for these very simple and obvious reasons that the parliamentary debates are read on this side of the water in preference to the congressional debates. They affect the ministers, who are very conspicuous persons, and in whom, therefore, all the intelligent world is interested; and they determine the course of politics in a great empire. The season of a parliamentary debate is a great field day on which Liberals and Conservatives pit their full forces against each other, and people like to watch the issues of the contest.

Our congressional debates, on the contrary, have no tithe of this interest, because they have no tithe of such significance and importance. The committee reports, upon which the debates take place, are backed by neither party; they represent merely the recommendations of a small body of members belonging to both parties, and are quite as likely to divide the vote of the party to which the majority of the Committee belong as they are to meet with opposition from the other side of the chamber. If they are carried, it is no party triumph; if they are lost, it is no party discomfiture. They are no more than the proposals of a mixed Committee, and may be rejected without political inconvenience to either party or reproof to the Committee; just as they may be passed without compliment to the Committee or political advantage to either side of the House. Neither party has any great stake in the controversy. The only importance that can attach to the vote must hang upon its relation to the next general election. If the report concern a question which is at the time so much in the public eye that all action upon it is likely to be marked and remembered against the day of popular action, parties are careful to vote as solidly as possible on what they conceive to be the safe side; but all other reports are disposed of without much thought of their influence upon the fortunes of distant elections, because that influence is remote and problematical.

In a word, the national parties do not act in Congress under the restraint of a sense of immediate responsibility. Responsibility is spread thin; and no vote or debate can gather it. It rests not so much upon parties as upon individuals; and it rests upon individuals in no such way as would make it either just or efficacious to visit upon them the iniquity of any legislative act. Looking at government from a practical and business-like, rather than from a theoretical and abstractly-ethical point of view,—treating the business of government as a business,—it seems to be unquestionably and in a high degree desirable that all legislation should distinctly represent the action of parties as parties. I know that it has been proposed by enthusiastic, but not too practical, reformers to do away with parties by some legerdemain of governmental reconstruction, accompanied and supplemented by some rehabilitation, devoutly to be wished, of the virtues least commonly controlling in fallen human nature; but it seems to me that it would be more difficult and less desirable than these amiable persons suppose to conduct a government of the many by means of any other device than party organization, and that the great need is, not to get rid of parties, but to find and use some expedient by which they can be managed and made amenable from day to day to public opinion. Plainly this cannot be effected by punishing here and there a member of Congress who has voted for a flagrantly dishonest appropriation bill, or an obnoxious measure relating to the tariff. Unless the punishment can be extended to the party—if any such be recognizable—with which these members have voted, no advantage has been won for self-government, and no triumph has been gained by public opinion. It should be desired that parties should act in distinct organizations, in accordance with avowed principles, under easily recognized leaders, in order that the voters might be able to declare by their ballots, not only their condemnation of any past policy, by withdrawing all support from the party responsible for it; but also and particularly their will as to the future administration of the government, by bringing into power a party pledged to the adoption of an acceptable policy.

It is, therefore, a fact of the most serious consequence that by our system of congressional rule no such means of controlling legislation is afforded. Outside of Congress the organization of the national parties is exceedingly well-defined and tangible; no one could wish it, and few could imagine it, more so; but within Congress it is obscure and intangible. Our parties marshal their adherents with the strictest possible discipline for the purpose of carrying elections, but their discipline is very slack and indefinite in dealing with legislation. At least there is within Congress no *visible,* and therefore no *controllable* party organization. The only bond of cohesion is the caucus, which occasionally whips a party together for coöperative action against the time for casting its vote upon some critical question. There is always a majority and a minority, indeed, but the legislation of a session does not represent the policy of either; it is simply an aggregate of the bills recommended by Committees composed of members from both sides of the House, and it is known to be usually, not the work of the majority men upon the Committees, but compromise conclusions bearing some shade or tinge of each of the variously-colored opinions and wishes of the committee-men of both parties.

It is plainly the representation of both parties on the Committees that makes party responsibility indistinct and organized party action almost impossible. If the Committees were composed entirely of members of the majority, and were thus constituted representatives of the party in power, the whole course of congressional proceedings would unquestionably take on a very different aspect. There would then certainly be a compact opposition to face the organized majority. Committee reports would be taken to represent the views of the party in power, and, instead of the scattered, unconcerted opposition, without plan or leaders, which now sometimes subjects the propositions of the Committees to vexatious hindrances and delays, there would spring up debate under skillful masters of opposition, who could drill their partisans for effective warfare and give shape and meaning to the purposes of the minority. But of course there can be no such definite division of forces so long as the efficient machinery of legislation is in the hands of both parties at once; so long as the parties are mingled and harnessed together in a common organization.

It may be said, therefore, that very few of the measures which come before Congress are party measures. They are, at any rate, not brought in as party measures. They are indorsed by select bodies of members chosen with a view to constituting an impartial board of examination for the judicial and thorough consideration of each subject of legislation; no member of one of these Committees is warranted in revealing any of the disagreements of the committee-room or the proportions of the votes there taken; and no color is meant to be given to the supposition that the reports made are intended to advance any party interest. Indeed, only a very slight examination of the measures which originate with the Committees is necessary to show that most of them are framed with a view to securing their easy passage by giving them as neutral and inoffensive a character as possible. The manifest object is to dress them to the liking of all factions.

Under such circumstances, neither the failure nor the success of any policy inaugurated by one of the Committees can fairly be charged to the account of either party. The Committee acted honestly, no doubt, and as they thought best; and there can, of course, be no assurance that, by taking away its congressional majority from the party to which the greater number of the committee-men belong, a Committee could be secured which would act better or differently.

The conclusion of the whole matter is, then, that public opinion cannot be instructed or elevated by the debates of Congress, not only because there are few debates seriously undertaken by Congress, but principally because no one not professionally interested in the daily course of legislation cares to read what is said by the debaters when Congress does stop to talk, inasmuch as nothing depends upon the issue of the discussion. The ordinary citizen cannot be induced to pay much heed to the details, or even to the main principles, of lawmaking, unless something else more interesting than the law itself be involved in the pending decision of the law-makers. If the fortunes of a party or the power of a great political leader are staked upon the final vote, he will listen with the keenest interest to all that the principal actors may have to say, and absorb much instruction in so doing; but if no such things hang in the balance, he will not turn from his business to listen; and if the true issues are not brought out in eager public contests which catch his ear because of their immediate personal interest, but must be sought amidst the information which can be made complete only by reading scores of newspapers, he will certainly never find them or care for them, and there is small use in printing a "Record" which he will not read.

I know not how better to describe our form of government in a single phrase than by calling it a government by the chairmen of the Standing Committees of Congress. This disintegrate ministry, as it figures on the floor of the House of Representatives, has many peculiarities. In the first place, it is made up of the elders of the assembly; for, by custom, seniority in congressional service determines the bestowal of the principal chairmanships; in the second place, it is constituted of selfish and warring elements; for chairman fights against chairman for use of the time of the assembly, though the most part of them are inferior to the chairman of Ways and Means, and all are subordinate to the chairman of the Committee on Appropriations; in the third place, instead of being composed of the associated leaders of Congress, it consists of the dissociated heads of forty-eight "little legislatures" (to borrow Senator Hoar's apt name for the Committees); and, in the fourth place, it is instituted by appointment from Mr. Speaker, who is, by intention, the chief judicial, rather than the chief political, officer of the House.

It is highly interesting to note the extraordinary power accruing to Mr. Speaker through this pregnant prerogative of appointing the Standing Committees of the House. That power is, as it were, the central and characteristic inconvenience and anomaly of our constitutional system, and on that account excites both the curiosity and the wonder of the student of institutions. The most esteemed writers upon our Constitution have failed to observe, not only that the Standing Committees are the most essential machinery of our governmental system, but also that the Speaker of the House of Representatives is the most powerful functionary of that system. So sovereign is he within the wide sphere of his influence that one could wish for accurate knowledge as to the actual extent of his power. But Mr. Speaker's powers cannot be known accurately, because they vary with the character of Mr. Speaker. All Speakers have, of late years especially, been potent factors in legislation, but some have, by reason of greater energy or less conscience, made more use of their opportunities than have others.

The Speaker's privilege of appointing the Standing Committees is nearly as old as Congress itself. At first the House tried the plan of balloting for its more important Committees, ordering, in April, 1789, that the Speaker should appoint only those Committees which should consist of not more than three members; but less than a year's experience of this method of organizing seems to have furnished satisfactory proof of its impracticability, and in January, 1790, the present rule was adopted: that "All committees shall be appointed by the Speaker, unless otherwise specially directed by the House." The rules of one House of Representatives are not, however, necessarily the rules of the next. No rule lives save by biennial readoption. Each newly-elected House meets without rules for its governance, and amongst the first acts of its first session is usually the adoption of the resolution that the rules of its predecessor shall be its own rules, subject, of course, to such revisions as it may, from time to time, see fit to make. Mr. Speaker's power of appointment, accordingly, always awaits the passage of this resolution; but it never waits in vain, for no House, however foolish in other respects, has yet been foolish enough to make fresh trial of electing its Committees. That mode may do well enough for the cool and leisurely Senate, but it is not for the hasty and turbulent House.

It must always, of course, have seemed eminently desirable to all thoughtful and experienced men that Mr. Speaker should be no more than the judicial guide and moderator of the proceedings of the House, keeping apart from the heated controversies of party warfare, and exercising none but an impartial influence upon the course of legislation; and probably when he was first invested with the power of appointment it was thought possible that he could exercise that great prerogative without allowing his personal views upon questions of public policy to control or even affect his choice. But it must very soon have appeared that it was too much to expect of a man who had it within his power to direct affairs that he should subdue all purpose to do so, and should make all appointments with an eye to regarding every preference but his own; and when that did become evident, the rule was undoubtedly retained only because none better could be devised. Besides, in the early years of the Constitution the Committees were very far from having the power they now possess. Business did not then hurry too fast for discussion, and the House was in the habit of scrutinizing the reports of the Committees much more critically than it now pretends to do. It deliberated in its open sessions as well as in its private committee-rooms, and the functionary who appointed its committees was simply the nominator of its advisers, not, as is the Speaker of to-day, the nominor of its rulers.

It is plain, therefore, that the office of Speaker of the House of Representatives is in its present estate a constitutional phenomenon of the first importance, deserving a very thorough and critical examination. If I have succeeded, in what I have already said, in making clear the extraordinary power of the Committees in directing legislation, it may now go without the saying that he who appoints those Committees is an autocrat of the first magnitude. There could be no clearer proof of the great political weight of the Speaker's high commission in this regard than the keen strife which every two years takes place over the election to the speakership, and the intense interest excited throughout the country as to the choice to be made. Of late years, the newspapers have had almost as much to say about the rival candidates for that office as about the candidates for the presidency itself, having come to look upon the selection made as a sure index of the policy to be expected in legislation.

The Speaker is of course chosen by the party which commands the majority in the House, and it has sometimes been the effort of scheming, self-seeking men of that majority to secure the elevation of some friend or tool of their own to that office, from which he can render them service of the most substantial and acceptable sort. But, although these intrigues have occasionally resulted in the election of a man of insignificant parts and doubtful character, the choice has usually fallen upon some representative party man of well-known antecedents and clearly-avowed opinions; for the House cannot, and will not willingly, put up with the intolerable inconvenience of a weak Speaker, and the majority are urged by self-respect and by all the weightiest considerations of expediency, as well as by a regard for the interests of the public business, to place one of their accredited leaders in the chair. If there be differences of opinion within the party, a choice between leaders becomes a choice between policies and assumes the greatest significance. The Speaker is expected to constitute the Committees in accordance with his own political views, and this or that candidate is preferred by his party, not at all because of any supposed superiority of knowledge of the precedents and laws of parliamentary usage, but because of his more popular opinions concerning the leading questions of the day.

Mr. Speaker, too, generally uses his powers as freely and imperatively as he is expected to use them. He unhesitatingly acts as the legislative chief of his party, organizing the Committees in the interest of this or that policy, not covertly and on the sly, as one who does something of which he is ashamed, but openly and confidently, as one who does his duty. Nor does his official connection with the Committees cease upon their appointment. It is his care to facilitate their control of the business of the House, by recognizing during the consideration of a report only those members with whom the reporting committee-man has agreed to share his time, and by keeping all who address the House within the strictest letter of the rules as to the length of their speeches, as well as by enforcing all those other restrictions which forbid independent action on the part of individual members. He must see to it that the Committees have their own way. In so doing he is not exercising arbitrary powers which circumstances and the habits of the assembly enable him safely to arrogate; he is simply enforcing the plain letter and satisfying the evident spirit of the rules.

A student of Roman law and institutions, looking at the Rules of the House of Representatives through glasses unaccustomed to search out aught but antiquities, might be excused for claiming that he found in the customs of the House a striking reproduction of Roman legislative methods. The Roman assembly, he would remind us, could not vote and debate at the same time; it had no privileges of amendment, but had to adopt every law as a whole or reject it as a whole; and no private member had a right to introduce a bill, that being the exclusive prerogative of the magistrates. But though he might establish a parallel satisfactory to himself between the magistrates of Rome and the Committees at Washington, and between the undebatable, unamendable laws of the ancient, and the undebated, unamended laws of the modern, republic, he could hardly find in the later system that compensating advantage which scholars have noted as giving to Roman legislation a clearness and technical perfection such as is to be found in one of the modern codes. Since Roman laws could not be amended in their passage, and must carry their meaning plainly to the comprehension of the commons, clear and brief drafting was cultivated as of the first necessity in drawing up measures which were first to gain popular approval and then to succeed or fail in accomplishing their ends according as they proved workable or impracticable.

No such comparison of our own with other systems can, however, find any favor in the eyes of a certain class of Americans who pride themselves upon being nothing if not patriotic, and who can consequently find no higher praise for the peculiar devices of committee government than that they are our own invention. "An ill-favored thing, sir, but mine own." No one will readily believe, however, that congressmen—even those of them who belong to this dutiful class—cherish a very loving admiration for the discipline to which they are nowadays subjected. As the accomplished librarian of Congress has declared, "the general conviction may be said to exist, that, under the great control over legislation and current business by the Speaker, and by the powerful Committee on Appropriations, combined with the rigor of the Rules of the House, there is less and less opportunity for individual members to make any influential mark in legislation. Independence and ability are repressed under the tyranny of the rules, and practically the power of the popular branch of Congress is concentrated in the Speaker and a few—very few—expert parliamentarians." And of course members of Congress see this. "We have but three forces in this House," exclaimed a jocose member from the Pacific coast, "the Brahmins of the Committee of Ways and Means—not the brains but the Brahmins of the House; the white-button mandarins of the Appropriations Committee; the dignified oligarchy called the Committee on Rules; the Speaker of the House; and the illustrious gentleman from Indiana." Naturally all men of independent spirit chafe under the arbitrary restraints of such a system, and it would be much more philosophical to conclude that they let it stand because they can devise nothing better, than that they adhere to its inconvenient practices because of their admiration for it as an American invention.

However that may be, the number of those who misuse the rules is greater than the number of those who strive to reform them. One of the most startling of the prevalent abuses is the hasty passage of bills under a suspension of the rules, a device "by means of which," says Senator Hoar, "a large proportion, perhaps the majority, of the bills which pass the House are carried through." This practice may be very clearly understood by following further Mr. Hoar's own words: "Every Monday after the morning hour, and at any time during the last ten days of a session, motions to suspend the rules are in order. At these times any member may move to suspend the rules and pass any proposed bill. It requires two thirds of the members voting to adopt such a motion. Upon it no debate or amendment is in order. In this way, if two thirds of the body agree, a bill is by a single vote, without discussion and without change, passed throught all the necessary stages, and made a law, so far as the House of Representatives can accomplish it; and in this mode hundreds of measures of vital importance receive, near the close of an exhausting session, without being debated, amended, printed, or understood, the constitutional assent of the representatives of the American people."

One very obvious comment to be made upon habits of procedure so palpably pernicious is, that nothing could be more natural under rules which repress individual action with so much stringency. Then, too, the mills of the Committees are known to grind slowly, and a very quick and easy way of getting rid of minor items of business is to let particular bills, of apparently innocent meaning or laudable intent, run through without commitment. There must be some outlet, too, through which the waters of delayed and accumulated business may be drained off as the end of a session draws near. Members who know how to take the House at an indulgent moment, and can in a few words make out a *primâ facie* case for the action they urge, can almost always secure a suspension of the rules.

To speak very plainly, it is wonderful that under such a system of government legislation is not oftener at sixes and sevens than it actually is. The infinitely varied and various interests of fifty millions of active people would be hard enough to harmonize and serve, one would think, were parties efficiently organized in the pursuit of definite, steady, consistent policies; and it is therefore simply amazing to find how few outrageously and fatally foolish, how few bad or disastrous, things have been done by means of our disintegrate methods of legislation. The Committees of the House to whom the principal topics of legislation are allotted number more than thirty. We are ruled by a score and a half of "little legislatures." Our legislation is conglomerate, not homogeneous. The doings of one and the same Congress are foolish in pieces and wise in spots. They can never, except by accident, have any common features. Some of the Committees are made up of strong men, the majority of them of weak men; and the weak are as influential as the strong. The country can get the counsel and guidance of its ablest representatives only upon one or two subjects; upon the rest it must be content with the impotent service of the feeble. Only a very small part of its most important business can be done well; the system provides for having the rest of it done miserably, and the whole of it taken together done at haphazard. There could be no more interesting problem in the doctrine of chances than that of reckoning the probabilities of there being any common features of principle in the legislation of an opening session. It might lighten and divert the leisure of some ingenious mathematician to attempt the calculation.

It was probably some such reflections as these which suggested the proposal, made not long since in the House, that there should be appointed, along with the usual Standing Committees, a new committee which should be known as the Executive Committee of the House, and should be empowered to examine and sort all the bills reported favorably by the other Standing Committees, and bring them forward in what might seem to it the order of their importance; a committee which should, in short, digest pending measures and guide the House in arranging its order of business. But it is seriously to be doubted whether such an addition to the present organization would do more than tighten the tyranny of committee rule and still further restrict freedom of debate and action. A committee to superintend committees would add very little to the efficiency of the House, and would certainly contribute nothing towards unifying legislation, unless the new committee were to be given the power, not yet thought of, of revising the work of the present Standing Committees. Such an executive committee is not quite the device needed.

Apparently committee government is but one of many experiments in the direction of the realization of an idea best expressed— so far as my reading shows—by John Stuart Mill; and is too much like other experiments to be quite as original and unique as some people would like to believe. There is, said Mr. Mill, a "distinction between the function of *making* laws, for which a numerous popular assembly is radically unfit, and that of *getting good laws made,* which is its proper duty, and cannot be satisfactorily fulfilled by any other authority"; and there is, consequently, "need of a legislative commission, as a permanent part of the constitution of a free country; consisting of a small number of highly-trained political minds, on whom, when parliament has determined that a law shall be made, the task of making it should be devolved; parliament retaining the power of passing or rejecting the bill when drawn up, but not of altering it otherwise than by sending proposed amendments to be dealt with by the commission." [7] It would seem, as I have said, that committee government is one form of the effort, now making by all self-governing peoples, to set up a satisfactory legislative commission somewhat after this order; and it might appear to some as if the proposed executive committee were a slight approximation to that form of the effort which is typified in the legislative functions of the British cabinet. It cannot, of course, be claimed that the forty-eight legislative commissions of the House of Representatives always answer the purpose when the House wants to get good laws made, or that each of them consists invariably of "a small number of highly-trained political minds"; but everybody sees that to say that they fall short of realizing the ideal would be nothing less than hypercritical.

In saying that our committee government has, germinally, some of the features of the British system, in which the ministers of the crown, the cabinet, are chosen from amongst the leaders of the parliamentary majority, and act not only as advisers of the sovereign but also as the great standing committee or "legislative commission" of the House of Commons, guiding its business and digesting its graver matters of legislation, I mean, of course, only that both systems represent the common necessity of setting apart some small body, or bodies, of legislative guides through whom a "big meeting" may get laws made. The difference between our device and the British is that we have a Standing Committee, drawn from both parties, for the consideration of each topic of legislation, whereas our English cousins have but a single standing committee that is charged with the origination of legislation,—a committee composed of the men who are recognized as the leaders of the party dominant in the state, and who serve at the same time as the political heads of the executive departments of the government.

The British system is perfected party government. No effort is made in the Commons, such as is made in the House of Representatives in the composition of the Committees, to give the minority a share in law-making. Our minorities are strongly represented on the Standing Committees; the minority in the Commons is not represented at all in the cabinet. It is this feature of closely organized party government, whereby the responsibility for legislation is saddled upon the majority, which, as I have already pointed out, gives to the debates and action of parliament an interest altogether denied to the proceedings of Congress. All legislation is made a contest for party supremacy, and if legislation goes wrong, or the majority becomes discontented with the course of policy, there is nothing for it but that the ministers should resign and give place to the leaders of the Opposition, unless a new election should procure for them a recruited following. Under such a system mere silent voting is out of the question; debate is a primary necessity. It brings the representatives of the people and the ministers of the Crown face to face. The principal measures of each session originate with the ministers, and embody the policy of the administration. Unlike the reports of our Standing Committees, which are intended to be simply the digested substance of the more sensible bills introduced by private members, the bills introduced into the House of Commons by the cabinet embody the definite schemes of the government; and the fact that the Ministry is made up of the leaders of the majority and represents always the principles of its party, makes the minority only the more anxious to have a chance to criticise its proposals. Cabinet government is a device for bringing the executive and legislative branches into harmony and co-operation without uniting or confusing their functions. It is as if the majority in the Commons deputized its leaders to act as the advisers of the Crown and the superintendents of the public business, in order that they might have the advantage of administrative knowledge and training in advising legislation and drafting laws to be submitted to parliament. This arrangement enlists the majority in behalf of successful administration without giving the ministers any power to coerce or arbitrarily influence legislative action. Each session of the Lords and Commons becomes a grand inquest into the affairs of the empire. The two estates sit as it were in committee on the management of the public business—sit with open doors, and spare themselves no fatigue in securing for every interest represented a full, fair, and impartial hearing.

It is evident why public debate is the very breath of life to such a system. The Ministry's tenure of office depends upon the success of the legislation they urge. If any of their proposals are negatived by parliament, they are bound to accept their defeat as an intimation that their administration is no longer acceptable to the party they represent, and are expected to resign, or to appeal, if they prefer, to the country for its verdict, by exercising their privilege of advising the sovereign to dissolve parliament and issue writs for a new election. It is, consequently, inevitable that the Ministry should be subjected to the most determined attacks and the keenest criticisms of the Opposition, and should be every day of the session put to the task of vindicating their course and establishing anew their claim to the confidence of their party. To shrink from discussion woud be to confess weakness; to suffer themselves to be worsted in discussion would be seriously to imperil their power. They must look to it, therefore, not only that their policy be defensible, but that it be valiantly defended also.

As might be expected, then, the Ministry seldom find the task of leading the House an easy one. Their plans are kept under an unceasing fire of criticism from both sides of the House; for there are independent sharp-shooters behind the ministers as well as heavy batteries in front of them; and there are many amongst their professed followers who give aid and comfort to the enemy. There come ever and again showers of stinging questions, too, from friends and foes alike, —questions great and small, direct and indirect, pertinent and impertinent, concerning every detail of administration and every tendency of policy.

But, although the initiative in legislation and the general direction of the business of parliament are the undisputed prerogatives of "the government," as the Ministry is called, they have not, of course, all the time of the House at their disposal. During the session, certain days of each week are set apart for the introduction and debate of bills brought in by private members, who, at the opening of the session, draw lots to decide the precedence of their bills or motions on the orders of the day. If many draw, those who get last choice of time find the session near its end, and private members' days being absorbed by belated government measures, before their opportunity has come, and must content themselves with hoping for better fortune next year; but time is generally found for a very fair and full consideration of a large number of private members' bills, and no member is denied a chance to air his favorite opinions in the House or to try the patience of his fellow-members by annual repetitions of the same proposition. Private members generally find out by long experience, however, that they can exert a more telling influence upon legislation by pressing amendments to government schemes, and can effect more immediate and satisfactory results by keeping the Ministry constantly in mind of certain phases of public opinion, than they could hope to exert or effect by themselves introducing measures upon which their party might hesitate to unite. Living as he does under a system which makes it the minister's wisest policy to allow the utmost freedom of debate, each member can take as prominent a part in the proceedings of the House as his abilities give him title to take. If he have anything which is not merely frivolous to say, he will have repeated opportunities to say it; for the Commons cough down only the bores and the talkers for the sake of talk.

The House of Commons, as well as our House of Representatives, has its committees, even its standing committees, but they are of the old-fashioned sort which merely investigate and report, not of the new American type which originate and conduct legislation. Nor are they appointed by the Speaker. They are chosen with care by a "Committee of Selection" composed of members of both parties. The Speaker is kept carefully apart from politics in all his functions, acting as the impartial, judicial president of the body. "Dignity of presence, courtliness of manner, great physical endurance, courage and impartiality of judgment, a consummate tact, and familiarity, 'born of life-long experience,' with the written and unwritten laws of the House,"—such are the qualities of the ideal Speaker. When he takes the chair he turns his back on partisan alliances and serves both parties alike with even hand. Such are the traditions of the office that its occupant feels himself as strictly bound to unbiased judgment as is the chiefest judge of the realm; and it has become no uncommon thing for a Speaker of tried ability to preside during several successive Parliaments, whether the party to whose suffrages he originally owed his elevation remains in power or no. His political principles do not affect his fitness for judicial functions.

The Commons in session present an interesting picture. Constrained by their habits of debate to sit in quarters suitable for the purpose, they crowd together in a hall of somewhat cramped proportions. It seems a place fit for hand to hand combats. The cushioned benches on which the members sit rise in close series on either side of a wide central aisle which they face. At one end of this aisle is raised the Speaker's chair, below and in front of which, invading the spaces of the aisle, are the desks of the wigged and gowned clerks. On the front benches nearest the Speaker and to his right sit the cabinet ministers, the leaders of the Government; opposite, on the front benches to the Speaker's left, sit the leaders of the Opposition. Behind and to the right of the ministers gather the majority; behind and to the left of their leaders, the minority. Above the rear benches and over the outer aisles of the House, beyond "the bar." hang deep galleries from which the outside world may look down upon the eager contests of the two parties which thus sit face to face with only the aisle between them. From these galleries the fortunate listen to the words of leaders whose names fill the ear of the world.

The organization of the French Assembly is in the main similar to that of the British Commons. Its leaders are the executive officers of the government, and are chosen from the ranks of the legislative majority by the President of the Republic, much as English cabinets are chosen by English sovereigns. They too are responsible for their policy and the acts of their administration to the Chamber which they lead. They, like their British prototypes, are the executive committee of the legislative body, and upon its will their tenure of office depends.

It cannot be said, however, that the proceedings of the French Assembly very closely resemble those of the British Commons. In the hall of the Deputies there are no close benches which face each other, and no two homogeneous parties to strive for the mastery. There are parties and parties, factions and factions, coteries and coteries. There are Bonapartists and Legitimatists, Republicans and Clericals, stubborn reactionists and headlong radicals, stolid conservatives and vindictive destructionists. One hears of the Centre, the Right Centre and the Left Centre, the Right, the Left, the Extreme Right and the Extreme Left. Some of these are, of course, mere factions, mere groups of irreconcilables; but several of them are, on the other hand, numerous and powerful parties upon whose mutual attractions and repulsions depend the formation, the authority, and the duration of cabinets.

Of course, too, there is in a body so made up a great deal of combustible material which the slightest circumstance suffices to kindle into a sudden blaze. The Assembly would not be French if it were not always excitable and sometimes uproarious. Absolute turbulence is so probable a contingency in its economy that a very simple and quickly applicable device is provided for its remedy. Should the deputies lose their heads altogether and become unmanageable, the President may *put on his hat,* and by that sign, unless calm be immediately restored, the sitting is adjourned for one hour, at the expiration of which time it is to be expected that the members may resume the business of the day in a cooler frame of mind. There are other rules of procedure observed in the Chamber which seem to foreign eyes at first sight very novel; but which upon closer examination may be seen to differ from some of the practices of our own House of Representatives in form rather than in essence. In France greater freedom of speech is allowed individual members than is possible under committee government, but recognition is not given to just any one who first gets the floor and catches the presiding officer's eye, as it is in the House of Commons, where none but the ministers are accorded any right of precedence in gaining a hearing. Those who wish to speak upon any pending question "inscribe" their names beforehand on a list in the keeping of the President, and the discussion is usually confined to those members who have "inscribed." When this list has been exhausted, the President takes the sense of the Chamber as to whether the debate shall be closed. The Chamber need not wait, however, to hear all the gentlemen who have put their names upon the list. If *une portion notable* of it tires sooner of the discussion or thinks itself sufficiently informed before all who wish to inform it have spoken, it may demand that the debate be brought to an end. Of course such a demand will not be heeded if it come from only a few isolated members, and even *une portion notable* may not interrupt a speaker with this peremptory call for what we should denominate the previous question, but which the French parliamentarian knows as the *clôture*. A demand for the *clôture* is not debatable. One speech may be made against it, but none in its favor. Unless it meet with very powerful resistance, it is expected to go through of its own weight. Even the *clôture*, however, must give way if a member of the Ministry claims the right to speak; for a minister must always be heard, and after he has spoken, moreover, there must always be allowed one speech in reply. Neither can the *clôture* be pronounced unless a majority of the deputies are present; and in case of doubt as to the will of the Chamber in the matter, after two votes have been taken without eliciting a full-voiced and indubitable assent, the discussion is tacitly suffered to proceed.

These rules are not quite so compulsive and inexorable as are those which sustain the government of our Standing Committees, nor do they seem quite imperative enough for the effectual governance of rampant deputies in their moments of wildest excitement; but they are somewhat more rigid than one would expect to find under a system of ministerial responsibility, the purity of whose atmosphere depends so directly upon a free circulation of debate. They are meant for a body of peculiar habits and a fiery temperament,—a body which is often brought screaming to its feet by the words of a passionate speaker, which is time and again betrayed into stormy disquiet, and which is ever being blown about by every passing wind of excitement. Even in its minor points of observance, the Chamber is essentially un-English. Members do not speak from their seats, as we are accustomed to see members of our public assemblies do, but from the "tribune," which is a conspicuous structure erected near the desks of the President and secretaries,—a box-like stand, closely resembling those narrow, quaintly-fashioned pulpits which are still to be seen in some of the oldest of our American churches. And since deputies must gain its commanding top before they may speak, there are said to be many exciting races for this place of vantage. Sometimes, indeed, very unseemly scenes take place, when several deputies, all equally eager to mount the coveted stand, reach its narrow steps at the same moment and contest the privilege of precedence,—especially if their friends rally in numbers to their assistance.

The British House of Commons and the French Chamber, though so unlike in the elements which compose them, and so dissimilar in their modes of procedure, are easily seen to be alike in constitutional significance, being made close kin by the principle of cabinet government, which they both recognize and both apply in its fullest efficacy. In both England and France a ministry composed of the chief officers of the executive departments are constituted at once the leaders of legislation and the responsible heads of administration,—a binding link between the legislative and executive branches of the government. In this regard these two systems present a strong contrast to our own. They recognize and support simple, straightforward, inartificial party government, under a standing committee of responsible party leaders, bringing legislature and executive side by side in intimate but open coöperation; whilst we, preferring to keep Congress and the departments at arm's length, permit only a less direct government by party majorities, checking party action by a complex legislative machinery of two score and eight composite, semi-ministerial Committees. The English take their parties straight,—we take ours mixed.

There is another aspect, however, in which all three of these systems are alike. They are alike in their essential purpose, which is to enable a mass meeting of representatives to superintend administration and get good laws made. Congress does not deal so directly with our executive as do the French and English parliaments with theirs, and cannot, therefore, control it quite so effectually; there is a great deal of friction amongst the many wheels of committee government; but, in the long run, Congress is quite as omnipotent as either the Chamber of Deputies or the House of Commons; and, whether there be two score committees with functions mainly legislative, or only one with functions half legislative, half executive, we have one form or another of something like Mr. Mill's "legislative commission."

THREE

The highest works of statesmanship require these three things: Great power in the minister, genius to counsel and support him, enlightenment in parliament to weigh and decide upon his plans.—PROFESSOR SEELEY.

When men are not acquainted with each other's principles, nor experienced in each other's talents, nor at all practiced in their mutual habitudes and dispositions by joint efforts of business; no personal confidence, no friendship, no common interest subsisting among them; it is evidently impossible that they can act a public part with uniformity, perseverance, or efficacy. —BURKE.

THE HOUSE OF REPRESENTATIVES

Revenue and Supply

"It requires," says Mr. Bagehot, "a great deal of time to have opinions," and if one is to judge from the legislative experience of some very enlightened nations, it requires more time to have opinions about finance than about any other subject. At any rate, very few nations have found time to have correct opinions about it. Governments which never consult the governed are usually content with very shabby, short-sighted methods of taxation,—with any methods, indeed, which can be made to yield the desired revenues without much trouble; and the agents of a self-governing people are quite sure to be too busy with elections and party management to have leisure to improve much upon the practices of autocrats in regard to this important care of administration. And yet this subject of finance seems to be interesting enough in a way. It is one of the commonplaces of our history that, ever since long before we came westward across the ocean, we have been readier to fight about taxation than about any other one thing,—than about a good many other things put together, indeed. There are several sadly bloody spots in the financial history of our race. It could probably be shown, however, if one cared to take time to show it, that it is easy to get vexed about mismanagement of the finances without knowing how they might be better managed. What we do not like is that we are taxed, —not that we are stupidly taxed. We do not need to be political economists to get angry about it; and when we have gotten angry about it in the past our rulers have not troubled themselves to study political economy in order to find out the best means of appeasing us. Generally they have simply shifted the burden from the shoulders of those who complained, and were able to make things unpleasant, to the shoulders of those who might complain, but could not give much trouble.

Of course there are some taxes which are much more hateful than others, and have on that account to be laid more circumspectly. All direct taxes are heartily disliked by every one who has to pay them, and as heartily abused, except by those who have never owned an ounce or an inch of property, and have never seen a tax-bill. The heart of the ordinary citizen regards them with an inborn aversion. They are so straightforward and peremptory in their demands. They soften their exactions with not a grain of consideration. The tax-collector, consequently, is never esteemed a lovable man. His methods are too blunt, and his powers too obnoxious. He comes to us, not with a "please," but with a "must." His requisitions always leave our pockets lighter and our hearts heavier. We cannot, for the life of us, help thinking, as we fold up his receipt and put it away, that government is much too expensive a luxury as nowadays conducted, and that that receipt is incontestable documentary proof of unendurable extortion. What we do not realize is, that life would be robbed of one of its chief satisfactions if this occasion of grumbling were to be taken away.

Indirect taxes, on the other hand, offend scarcely anybody.

It is one of the open secrets of finance that in almost every system of taxation the indirect overcrow the direct taxes by many millions, and have a knack for levying on the small resources of insignificant persons which direct taxes have never learned. They know how to coax pennies out of poor people whose names have never been on the tax-collector's books. But they are very sly, and have at command a thousand successful disguises. High or complicated tariffs afford them their most frequent and abundant opportunities. Most people have very short thoughts, which do not extend beyond the immediate phenomena of direct vision, and so do not recognize the hand of the government in the high prices charged them in the shops. Very few of us taste the tariff in our sugar; and I suppose that even very thoughtful topers do not perceive the license-tax in their whiskey. There is little wonder that financiers have always been nervous in dealing with direct, but confident and free of hand in laying indirect, taxes.

It may, therefore, be accounted one of the customary advantages which our federal government possesses over the governments of the States, that it has almost always, in ordinary times, derived its entire revenue from prompt and facile indirect taxes, whilst the States have had to live upon the tardy and begrudged income derivable from a direct levy. Since we have had to support two governments it has been wisely resolved to let us, as long as possible, feel the weight of only one of them,—and that the one which can get at us most readily, and, at the same time, be most easily and promptly controlled by our votes. It is a plain, convenient, and, on the whole, satisfactory division of domain, though the responsibility which it throws on state legislatures is more apt to pinch and prove vexatious than is that which it lays upon Congress. Mr. Gladstone, the greatest of English financiers, once playfully described direct and indirect taxes as two sisters,—daughters of Necessity and Invention,—"differing only as sisters may differ, . . . the one being more free and open, the other somewhat more shy, retiring, and insinuating"; and frankly owned that, whether from "a lax sense of moral obligation or not," he, as Chancellor of the Exchequer, "thought it not only allowable, but even an act of duty, to pay his addresses to them both." But our chancellors of the exchequer, the chairmen of the Committee of Ways and Means, are bound by other traditions of courtship, and have, besides, usually shown no susceptibility to the charms of the blunt and forward elder of these two sisters. They have been constant, even if now and again a little wayward, in their devotion to the younger.

I suppose that no one ever found the paths of finance less thorny and arduous than have our national publicists. If their tasks be compared with those of European and English financiers, it is plain to see that their lines have fallen in pleasant places. From almost the very first they have had boundless resources to draw upon, and they have certainly of late days had free leave to spend limitless revenues in what extravagances they pleased. It has come to be infinitely more trouble to spend our enormous national income than to collect it. The chief embarrassments have arisen, not from deficits, but from surpluses. It is very fortunate that such has been the case, because for the best management of the finances of a nation, when revenue is scant and economy imperative, it is absolutely necessary to have financial administration in the hands of a few highly-trained and skillful men acting subject to a very strict responsibility, and this is just what our committee system does not allow. As in other matters of legislation, so in finance, we have many masters acting under a very dim and inoperative accountability. Of course under such ministration our financial policy has always been unstable, and has often strayed very far from the paths of wisdom and providence; for even when revenue is superabundant and extravagance easy, irresponsible, fast and loose methods of taxation and expenditure must work infinite harm. The only difference is that during such times the nation is not so sensitive to the ill effects wrought by careless policy. Mismanagement is not generally blamed until a great many people have discovered it by being hurt by it. Meantime, however, it is none the less interesting and important to study our government, with a view to gauging its qualities and measuring accurately its capabilities for good or bad service; and the study can doubtless be much more dispassionately conducted before we have been seriously hurt by foolish, unsteady administration than afterwards. The forces of the wind can be reckoned with much more readily while they are blowing only a gale than after they have thrown a hurricane upon us.

The national income is controlled by one Committee of the House and one of the Senate; the expenditures of the government are regulated by fifteen Committees of the House and five of the Senate; and the currency is cared for by two Committees of the House and one of the Senate; by all of which it appears that the financial administration of the country is in the hands of twenty-four Committees of Congress,—a mechanism of numerous small and great functions, quite complex enough to be worth careful study, perhaps too complex to be studied directly without an aiding knowledge of some simpler system with which it may be compared. Our own budget may be more readily followed through all the vicissitudes of committee scrutiny, and all the varied fortunes of committee action, after one has traced some other budget through the simpler processes of some other system of government.

The British system is, perhaps, in its main features, the simplest in existence. It is, besides, the pattern after which the financial systems of the chief governments of Europe have been modeled, and which we have ourselves in a measure copied; so that by prefacing the study of other systems by a careful examination of the British, in its present form, one may start with the great advantage of knowing the characteristics of what may fairly be called the parent stock. Parliament, then, in the first place, simply controls, it does not originate, measures of financial administration. It acts through the agency and under the guidance of the ministers of the Crown. Early in each annual session "the estimates" are submitted to the Commons, which, when hearing such statements, sits in Committee of the Whole House, known as Committee of Supply. The estimates come before the House in truly formidable shape. Each department presents its estimates in a huge quarto volume, "crammed with figures and minute entries of moneys wanted for the forthcoming year." [1] But the House itself does not have to digest this various and overwhelming mass of figures. The digesting is done in the first instance by the official leaders of the House. "The ministers in charge of the naval and military services lay before the Committee [of Supply] their respective statements of the sums which will be required for the maintenance of those services; and somewhat later in the session a common estimate for the various civil services is submitted also." Those statements are, as it were, condensed synopses of the details of the quartos, and are made with the object of rendering quite clear to the House, sitting under the informal rules of Committee, the policy of the expenditures proposed and the correctness of the calculations upon which they are based. Any member may ask what pertinent questions he pleases of the minister who is making the statement, so that nothing needing elucidation may be passed by without full explanation. After the statement has been completed to the satisfaction of the Committee, a vote is taken, at the motion of the minister, upon each item of expenditure, and the duties of the Committee of Supply have been performed.

The estimates are always submitted "on the collective responsibility of the whole cabinet." "The army and navy estimates have, as a rule, been considered and settled in cabinet council before being submitted to the House; and the collective responsibility of the Ministry is in this case, therefore, not technical merely, but substantial." If the estimates are resisted and rejected by the Committee, the ministers, of course, resign. They "cannot acquiesce in a refusal on the part of parliament to sanction the expenditure which" they "have assumed the responsibility of declaring necessary for the support of the civil government, and the maintenance of the public credit at home and abroad." The votes in Committee of Supply are, therefore, vital in the history of every administration, being taken as sure indexes of the amount of confidence placed by the House in the government.

But the votes in Committee of Supply are only the first steps in parliament's annual supervision of the public finances. They are simply the spending votes. In order to consider the means by which money is to be raised to meet the outlays sanctioned by the Committee of Supply, the House resolves itself into Committee of the Whole, under the name of the Committee of Ways and Means. It is to this Committee that the Chancellor of the Exchequer submits his budget every year, on or soon

before the fifth of April, the date at which the national accounts are made up, the financial year closing on the thirty-
first of March. In order to prepare his budget, the Chancellor
must of course have early knowledge of the estimates made for
the various services. Several months, therefore, before the estimates are laid before the House in Committee of Supply, the
various departments are called upon by the Treasury to send
in statements of the sums required to defray the expenses of
the current year, and these estimates are carefully examined by
the Chancellor, with a view not only to exercising his duty of
keeping the expenditures within the limits of economy, but also
to ascertaining how much revenue he will have to secure in
order to meet the proper expenditure contemplated. He must
balance estimated needs over against estimated resources, and
advise the House in Committee of Ways and Means as to the
measures by which taxation is to be made to afford sufficient
revenue. Accordingly he calls in the aid of the permanent heads
of the revenue departments who furnish him with "their estimates of the public revenue for the ensuing year, upon the
hypothesis that taxation will remain unchanged."

Having with such aids made up his budget, the Chancellor
goes before the Committee of Ways and Means prepared to
give a clear history of the financial administration of the year
just closed, and to submit definite plans for adjusting the taxation and providing for the expected outlays of the year just
opening. The precedents of a wise policy of long standing forbid his proposing to raise any greater revenue than is absolutely
necessary for the support of the government and the maintenance of the public credit. He therefore never asks the Committee to lay taxes which promise a considerable surplus. He
seeks to obtain only such an overplus of income as will secure
the government against those slight errors of underestimation
of probable expenses or of overestimation of probable revenue
as the most prudent of administrations is liable to make. It
the estimated revenue considerably exceed the estimated expenses, he proposes such remissions of taxation as will bring
the balance as near equality as prudence will permit; if the
anticipated expenses run beyond the figure of the hoped-for
revenue, he asks that certain new taxes be laid, or that certain

existing taxes be increased; if the balance between the two sides of the forecast account shows a pretty near approach to equilibrium, so the scale of revenue be but a little the heavier of the two, he contents himself with suggesting such a readjustment of existing taxes as will be likely to distribute the burden of taxation more equitably amongst the tax-paying classes, or facilitate hampered collections by simplifying the complex methods of assessment and imposition.

Such is the budget statement to which the House of Commons listens in Committee of Ways and Means. This Committee may deal with the proposals of the Chancellor of the Exchequer with somewhat freer hand than the Committee of Supply may use in passing upon the estimates. The Ministry is not so stiffly insistent upon having its budget sanctioned as it is upon having its proposed expenditures approved. It is understood to pledge itself to ask for no more money than it honestly needs; but it simply advises with the House as to the best way of raising that money. It is punctiliously particular about being supplied with the funds it asks for, but not quite so exacting as to the ways and means of supply. Still, no Ministry can stand if the budget be rejected out of hand, or if its demands for the means of meeting a deficiency be met with a flat refusal, no alternative means being suggested by the Opposition. Such votes would be distinct declarations of a want of confidence in the Ministry, and would of course force them to resign.

The Committee of Ways and Means, then, carries out, under the guidance of the Chancellor of the Exchequer, the resolutions of the Committee of Supply. The votes of the latter Committee, authorizing the expenditures mapped out in the estimates, are embodied in "a resolution proposed in Committee of Ways and Means for a general grant out of the Consolidated Fund 'towards making good the supply granted to Her Majesty;' " and that resolution, in order that it may be prepared for the consideration of the House of Lords and the Crown, is afterwards cast by the House into the form of a Bill, which passes through the regular stages and in due course becomes law. The proposals of the Chancellor of the Exchequer with reference to changes in taxation are in like manner embodied in resolutions in Committee of Ways and Means, and subsequently, upon the report of the Committee, passed by the House in the shape of Bills, "Ways and Means Bills" generally pass the Lords without trouble. The absolute control of the Commons over the subjects of revenue and supply has been so long established that the upper House would not now dream of disputing it; and as the power of the Lords is simply a privilege to accept or reject a money bill as a whole, including no right to amend, the peers are wont to let such bills go through without much scrutiny.

But so far I have spoken only of that part of parliament's control of the finances which concerns the future. The "Ways and Means Bills" provide for coming expenses and a prospective revenue. Past expenses are supervised in a different way. There is a double process of audit by means of a special Audit Department of the Civil Service, which is, of course, a part of the permanent organization of the administration, having it in charge "to examine the accounts and vouchers of the entire expenditure," and a special committee nominated each year by the House "to audit the Audit Department." This committee is usually made up of the most experienced business men in the Commons, and before it "all the accounts of the completed financial year are passed in review." "Minute inquiries are occasionally made by it into the reasons why certain items of expenditure have occurred; it discusses claims for compensation, grants, and special disbursements, in addition to the ordinary outgoings of the department, mainly, to be sure, upon the information and advice of the departments themselves, but still with a certain independence of view and judgment which must be valuable."

The strictness and explicitness with which the public accounts are kept of course greatly facilitate the process of audit. The balance which is struck on the thirty-first of every March is of the most definite sort. It deals only with the actual receipts and disbursements of the completed fiscal year. At that date all unexpended credits lapse. If the expenditure of certain sums has been sanctioned by parliamentary vote, but some of the granted moneys remain undrawn when April comes in, they can be used only after a regrant by the Commons. There are, therefore, no unclosed accounts to obscure the view of the auditing authorities. Taxes and credits have the same definite period, and there are no arrears or unexpended balances to confuse the book-keeping. The great advantages of such a system in the way of checking extravagances which would otherwise be possible, may be seen by comparing it with the system in vogue in France, in whose national balance-sheet "arrears of taxes in one year overlap with those of other years," and "credits old jostle credits new," so that it is said to be "always three or four years before the nation can know what the definitive expenditure of a given year is."

For the completion of this sketch of financial administration under the Commons it is of course necessary to add a very distinct statement of what I may call the *accessibility* of the financial officers of the government. They are always present to be questioned. The Treasury department is, as becomes its importance, exceptionally well represented in the House. The Chancellor of the Exchequer, the working chief of the department, is invariably a member of the Commons, "and can be called to account by interrogation or motion with respect to all matters of Treasury concern"—with respect, that is, to well-nigh "the whole sphere of the discipline and economy of the Executive Government"; for the Treasury has wide powers of supervision over the other departments in all matters which may in any way involve an outlay of public money. "And not only does the invariable presence of the Chancellor of the Exchequer in the House of Commons make the representation of that department peculiarly direct, but, through the Secretary of the Treasury, and, with respect to certain departmental matters, through the Junior Lords, the House possesses peculiar facilities for ascertaining and expressing its opinion upon the details of Treasury administration." It has its responsible servants always before it, and can obtain what glimpses it pleases into the inner workings of the departments which it wishes to control.

It is just at this point that our own system of financial administration differs most essentially from the systems of England, of the Continent, and of the British colonial possessions. Congress does not come into direct contact with the financial officers of the government. Executive and legislature are separated by a hard and fast line, which sets them apart in what was meant to be independence, but has come to amount to isolation. Correspondence between them is carried on by means of written communications, which, like all formal writings, are vague, or by means of private examinations of officials in committee-rooms to which the whole House cannot be audience. No one who has read official documents needs to be told how easy it is to conceal the essential truth under the apparently candid and all-disclosing phrases of a voluminous and particularizing report; how different those answers are which are given with the pen from a private office from those which are given with the tongue when the speaker is looking an assembly in the face. It is sufficiently plain, too, that resolutions which call upon officials to give testimony before a committee are a much clumsier and less efficient means of eliciting information than is a running fire of questions addressed to ministers who are always in their places in the House to reply publicly to all interrogations. It is reasonable to conclude, therefore, that the House of Representatives is much less intimately acquainted with the details of federal Treasury affairs than is such a body as the House of Commons, with the particulars of management in the Treasury which it oversees by direct and constant communication with the chief Treasury officials.

This is the greater drawback in our system, because, as a further result of its complete separation from the executive, Congress has to originate and perfect the budget for itself. It does not hear the estimates translated and expounded in condensed statements by skilled officials who have made it their business, because it is to their interest, to know thoroughly what they are talking about; nor does it have the benefit of the guidance of a trained, practical financier when it has to determine questions of revenue. The Treasury is not consulted with reference to problems of taxation, and motions of supply are disposed of with no suggestions from the departments beyond an itemized statement of the amounts needed to meet the regular expenses of an opening fiscal year.

In federal book-keeping the fiscal year closes on the thirtieth of June. Several months before that year expires, however, the estimates for the twelve months which are to succeed are made ready for the use of Congress. In the autumn each department and bureau of the public service reckons its pecuniary needs for the fiscal year which is to begin on the following first of July (making explanatory notes, and here and there an interjected prayer for some unwonted expenditure, amongst the columns of figures), and sends the resulting document to the Secretary of the Treasury. These reports, including of course the estimates of the various bureaux of his own department, the Secretary has printed in a thin quarto volume of some three hundred and twenty-five pages, which for some reason or other, not quite apparent, is called a "Letter from the Secretary of the Treasury transmitting estimates of appropriations required for the fiscal year ending June 30," . . . and which boasts a very distinct arrangement under the heads Civil Establishment, Military Establishment, Naval Establishment, Indian Affairs, Pensions, Public Works, Postal Service, etc., a convenient summary of the chief items, and a complete index.

In December this "Letter" is sent, as a part of the Secretary of the Treasury's annual report to Congress, to the Speaker of the House of Representatives, immediately after the convening of that body, and is referred to the Standing Committee on Appropriations. The House itself does not hear the estimates read; it simply passes the thin quartos over to the Committee; though, of course, copies of it may be procured and studied by any member who chooses to scrutinize the staring pages of columned figures with the dutiful purpose of keeping an eye upon the uses made of the public revenue. Taking these estimates into consideration, the Committee on Appropriations found upon them the "general appropriation bills," which the rules require them to report to the House "within thirty days after their appointment, at every session of Congress, commencing on the first Monday in December," unless they can give satisfactory reasons in writing for not doing so. The "general appropriation bills" provide separately for legislative, executive, and judicial expenses; for sundry civil expenses; for consular and diplomatic expenses; for the Army; for the Navy; for the expenses of the Indian department; for the payment of invalid and other pensions; for the support of the Military Academy; for fortifications; for the service of the Post-Office department, and for mail transportation by ocean steamers.

It was only through the efforts of a later-day spirit of vigilant economy that this practice of making the appropriations for each of the several branches of the public service in a separate bill was established. During the early years of the Constitution very loose methods of appropriation prevailed. All the moneys for the year were granted in a single bill, entitled "An Act making Appropriations for the support of the Government"; and there was no attempt to specify the objects for which they were to be spent. The gross sum given could be applied at the discretion of the heads of the executive departments, and was always large enough to allow much freedom in the undertaking of new schemes of administration, and in the making of such additions to the clerical force for the different offices as might seem convenient to those in control. It was not until 1862 that the present practice of somewhat minutely specifying the uses to be made of the funds appropriated was reached, though Congress had for many years been by slow stages approaching such a policy. The history of appropriations shows that "there has been an increasing tendency to limit the discretion of the executive departments, and bring the details of expenditure more immediately under the annual supervision of Congress"; a tendency which has specially manifested itself since the close of the recent war between the States.[2] In this, as in other things, the appetite for government on the part of Congress has grown with that perfection of organization which has rendered the gratification of its desire for power easily attainable. In this matter of appropriations, however, increased care has unquestionably resulted in a very decided curtailment of extravagance in departmental expenditure, though Congress has often shown a blind ardor for retrenchment which has fallen little short of parsimony, and which could not have found place in its legislation had it had such adequate means of confidential communication with the executive departments as would have enabled it to understand their real needs, and to discriminate between true economy and those scant allowances which only give birth to deficiencies, and which, even under the luckiest conditions, serve only for a very brief season to create the impression which they are usually meant to beget,—that the party in power is the party of thrift and honesty, seeing in former appropriations too much that was corrupt and spendthrift, and desiring to turn to the good ways of wisdom and frugality.

There are some portions of the public expenditure which do not depend upon the annual gifts of Congress, but which are provided for by statutes which run without limit of date. These are what are known as the "permanent appropriations." They cover, on the one hand, such indeterminate charges as the interest on the public debt, the amounts annually paid into the sinking fund, the outlays of refunding, the interest on the bonds issued to the Pacific Railways; and, on the other hand, such specific charges as the maintenance of the militia service, the costs of the collection of the customs revenue, and the interest on the bequest to the Smithsonian Institution. Their aggregate sum constitutes no insignificant part of the entire public expense. In 1880, in a total appropriation of about $307,000,000, the permanent appropriations fell short of the annual grant by only about sixteen and a half millions. In later years, however, the proportion has been smaller, one of the principal items, the interest on the public debt, becoming, of course, continually less as the debt is paid off, and other items reaching less amounts, at the same time that the figures of the annual grants have risen rather than fallen.

With these permanent grants the Committee on Appropriations has, of course, nothing to do, except that estimates of the moneys to be drawn under authority of such grants are submitted to its examination in the Secretary of the Treasury's "Letter," along with the estimates for which special appropriations are asked. Upon these latter estimates the general appropriations are based. The Committee may report its bills at any stage of the House's business, provided only that it does not interrupt a member who is speaking; and these bills when reported may at any time, by a majority vote, be made a special order of the day. Of course their consideration is the most imperative business of the session. They must be passed before the end of June, else the departments will be left altogether without means of support. The chairman of the Committee on Appropriations is, consequently, a very masterful authority in the House. He can force it to a consideration of the business of his Committee at almost any time; and by withholding his reports until the session is well advanced can crowd all other topics from the docket. For much time is spent over each of the "general appropriation bills." The spending of money is one of the two things that Congress invariably stops to talk about; the other being the raising of money. The talk is made always in Committee of the Whole, into which the House at once resolves itself whenever appropriations are to be considered. While members of this, which may be called the House's Committee of Supply, representatives have the freest opportunity of the session for activity, for usefulness, or for meddling, outside the sphere of their own committee work. It is true that the "five-minutes' rule" gives each speaker in Committee of the Whole scant time for the expression of his views, and that the House can refuse to accord full freedom of debate to its other self, the Committee of the Whole, by limiting the time which it is to devote to the discussion of matters referred to it, or by providing for its discharge from the further consideration of any bill committed to it, after it shall have acted without debate on all amendments pending or that may be offered; but as a rule every member has a chance to offer what suggestions he pleases upon questions of appropriation, and many hours are spent in business-like debate and amendment of such bills, clause by clause and item by item. The House learns pretty thoroughly what is in each of its appropriation bills before it sends it to the Senate.

But, unfortunately, the dealings of the Senate with money bills generally render worthless the painstaking action of the House. The Senate has been established by precedent in the very freest possible privileges of amendment as regards these bills no less than as regards all others. The Constitution is silent as to the origination of bills appropriating money. It says simply that "all bills for *raising revenue* shall originate in the House of Representatives," and that in considering these "the Senate may propose or concur with amendments as on other bills" (Art. I., Sec. VII.); but, "by a practice as old as the

Government itself, the constitutional prerogative of the House has been held to apply to all the general appropriation bills," [3] and the Senate's right to amend these has been allowed the widest conceivable scope. The upper house may add to them what it pleases; may go altogether outside of their original provisions and tack to them entirely new features of legislation, altering not only the amounts but even the objects of expenditure, and making out of the materials sent them by the popular chamber measures of an almost totally new character. As passed by the House of Representatives, appropriation bills generally provide for an expenditure considerably less than that called for by the estimates; as returned from the Senate, they usually propose grants of many additional millions, having been brought by that less sensitive body up almost, if not quite, to the figures of the estimates.

After passing their ordeal of scrutiny and amendment in the Senate, the appropriation bills return with their new figures to the House. But when they return it is too late for the House to put them again into the crucible of Committee of the Whole. The session, it may be taken for granted, was well on towards its middle age before they were originally introduced by the House Committee on Appropriations; after they reached the Senate they were referred to its corresponding Committee; and the report of that Committee upon them was debated at the leisurely length characteristic of the weightier proceedings of the upper chamber; so that the last days of the session are fast approaching when they are sent down to the House with the work of the Senate's hand upon them. The House is naturally disinclined to consent to the radical alterations wrought by the Senate, but there is no time to quarrel with its colleague, unless it can make up its mind to sit through the heat of midsummer, or to throw out the bill and accept the discomforts of an extra session. If the session be the short one, which ends, by constitutional requirement, on the 4th of March, the alternative is the still more distasteful one of leaving the appropriations to be made by the next House.

The usual practice, therefore, is to adjust such differences by means of a conference between the two Houses. The House rejects the Senate's amendments without hearing them read;

the Senate stoutly refuses to yield; a conference ensues, conducted by a committee of three members from each chamber; and a compromise is effected, by such a compounding of disagreeing propositions as gives neither party to the quarrel the victory, and commonly leaves the grants not a little below the amounts asked for by the departments. As a rule, the Conference Committee consists, on the part of the House, of the chairman of its Committee on Appropriations, some other well-posted member of that Committee, and a representative of the minority. Its reports are matters of highest prerogative. They may be brought in even while a member is speaking. It is much better to silence a speaker than to delay for a single moment, at this stage of the session, the pressing, imperious question of the supplies for the support of the government. The report is, therefore, acted upon immediately and in a mass, and is generally adopted without debate. So great is the haste that the report is passed upon before being printed, and without giving any one but the members of the Conference Committee time to understand what it really contains. There is no chance of remark or amendment. It receives at once sanction or rejection as a whole; and the chances are, of course, in favor of its being accepted, because to reject it would but force a new conference and bring fresh delays.

It is evident, therefore, that after all the careful and thoroughgoing debate and amendment of Committee of the Whole in the House, and all the grave deliberation of the Senate to which the general appropriations are subjected, they finally pass in a very chaotic state, full of provisions which neither the House nor the Senate likes, and utterly vague and unintelligible to every one save the members of the Conference Committee; so that it would seem almost as if the generous portions of time conscientiously given to their consideration in their earlier stages had been simply time thrown away.

The result of the under-appropriation to which Congress seems to have become addicted by long habit in dealing with the estimates, is, of course, the addition of another bill to the number of the regular annual grants. As regularly as the annual session opens there is a Deficiency Bill to be considered. Doubtless deficiencies frequently arise because of miscalculations or extravagance on the part of the departments; but the most serious deficiencies are those which result from the close-fistedness of the House Committee on Appropriations, and the compromise reductions which are wrung from the Senate by conference committees. Every December, consequently, along with the estimates for the next fiscal year, or at a later period of the session in special communications, come estimates of deficiencies in the appropriations for the current year, and the apparent economies of the grants of the preceding session have to be offset in the gifts of the inevitable Deficiency Bill. It is as if Congress had designedly established the plan of making semiannual appropriations. At each session it grants part of the money to be spent after the first of July following, and such sums as are needed to supplement the expenditures previously authorized to be made after the first of July preceding. It doles out their allowances in installments to its wards, the departments.

It is usual for the Appropriations Committees of both Houses, when preparing the annual bills, to take the testimony of the directing officers of the departments as to the actual needs of the public service in regard to all the principal items of expenditure. Having no place upon the floor of the House, and being, in consequence, shut out from making complete public statements concerning the estimates, the heads of the several executive departments are forced to confine themselves to private communications with the House and Senate Committees. Appearing before those Committees in person, or addressing them more formally in writing, they explain and urge the appropriations asked in the "Letter" containing the estimates. Their written communications, though addressed only to the chairman of one of the Committees, frequently reach Congress itself, being read in open session by some member of the Committee in order to justify or interpret the items of appropriation proposed in a pending bill. Not infrequently the head of a department exerts himself to secure desired supplies by dint of negotiation with individual members of the Committee, and by repeated and insistent private appeals to their chairman.

Only a very small part of the relations between the Committees and the departments is a matter of rule. Each time that the estimates come under consideration the Committees must specially seek, or the departments newly volunteer, information and advice. It would seem, however, that it is now less usual for the Committees to ask than for the Secretaries to offer counsel and suggestion. In the early years of the government it was apparently not uncommon for the chairman of spending committees to seek out departmental officials in order to get necessary enlightenment concerning the mysteries of the estimates, though it was often easier to ask for than to get the information wanted. An amusing example of the difficulties which then beset a committee-man in search of such knowledge is to be found in the private correspondence of John Randolph of Roanoke. Until 1865 the House Committee of Ways and Means, which is one of the oldest of the Standing Committees, had charge of the appropriations; it was, therefore, Mr. Randolph's duty, as chairman of that Committee in 1807, to look into the estimates, and he thus recounts, in an interesting and exceedingly characteristic letter to his intimate friend and correspondent, Nicholson, this pitiful experience which he had had in performing that duty: "I called some time since at the navy office to ask an explanation of certain items of the estimate for this year. The Secretary called upon his chief clerk, who knew very little more of the business than his master. I propounded a question to the head of the department; he turned to the clerk like a boy who cannot say his lesson, and with imploring countenance beseeches aid; the clerk with much assurance gabbled out some commonplace jargon, which I could not take for sterling; an explanation was required, and both were dumb. This pantomime was repeated at every item, until, disgusted and ashamed for the degraded situation of the principal, I took leave without pursuing the subject, seeing that my object could not be attained. There was not one single question relating to the department that the Secretary could answer." [4] It is to be hoped that the Secretaries of to-day are somewhat better versed in the affairs of their departments than was respectable Robert Smith, or, at any rate, that they have chief clerks who can furnish inquiring chairmen with something better than commonplace jargon which no shrewd man can take for sterling information; and it is altogether probable that such a scene as the one just described would nowadays be quite impossible. The book-keeping of later years has been very much stricter and more thorough than it was in the infancy of the departments; the estimates are much more thoroughly differentiated and itemized; and a minute division of labor in each department amongst a numerous clerical force makes it comparatively easy for the chief executive officers to acquaint themselves quickly and accurately with the details of administration. They do not wait, therefore, as a general thing, to be sought out and questioned by the Committees, but bestir themselves to get at the ears of the committee-men, and especially to secure, if possible, the influence of the chairmen in the interest of adequate appropriations.

These irregular and generally informal communications between the Appropriations Committees and the heads of the departments, taking the form sometimes of pleas privately addressed by the Secretaries to individual members of the Committees, and again of careful letters which find their way into the reports laid before Congress, stand in our system in the place of the annual financial statements which are in British practice made by the ministers to parliament, under circumstances which constitute very full and satisfactory public explanations and the freest replies to all pertinent questions invariable features of the supervision of the finances by the Commons. Our ministers make their statements to both Houses indirectly and piecemeal, through the medium of the Committees. They are mere witnesses, and are in no definite way responsible for the annual appropriations. Their secure four-year tenure of office is not at all affected by the treatment the estimates receive at the hands of Congress. To see our cabinet officers resign because appropriations had been refused for the full amount asked for in the Secretary of the Treasury's "Letter" would be as novel in our eyes as would be, in the view of our English cousins, the sight of a Ministry of the Crown remaining in office under similar circumstances. Indeed, were our cabinets to stake their positions upon the fortunes of the estimates submitted to Congress, we should probably suffer the tiresome inconvenience of yearly resignations; for even when the heads of the departments tax all their energies and bring into requisition all their arts of persuasion to secure ample grants from the Committees, the House Committee cuts down the sums as usual, the Senate Committee adds to them as before, and the Conference Committee strikes a deficient compromise balance according to time-honored custom.

There is in the House another appropriations committee besides the Committee on Appropriations. This is the Committee on Rivers and Harbors, created in December, 1883, by the Forty-eighth Congress, as a sharer in the too great prerogatives till then enjoyed by the Committee on Commerce. The Committee on Rivers and Harbors represents, of course, the lately-acquired permanency of the policy of internal improvements. Until 1870 that policy had had a very precarious existence. Strenuously denied all tolerance by the severely constitutional Presidents of the earlier days, it could not venture to declare itself openly in separate appropriations which offered an easy prey to the watchful veto, but skulked in the unobtrusive guise of items of the general grants, safe under the cover of respectable neighbor items. The veto has never been allowed to seek out single features in the acts submitted to the executive eye, and even such men as Madison and Monroe, stiff and peremptory as they were in the assertion of their conscientious opinions, and in the performance of what they conceived to be their constitutional duty, and much as they disapproved of stretching the Constitution to such uses as national aid to local and inland improvements, were fain to let an occasional gift of money for such purposes pass unforbidden rather than throw out the general appropriation bill to which it was tacked. Still, Congress did not make very frequent or very flagrant use of this trick, and schemes of internal improvement came altogether to a stand-still when faced by President Jackson's imperious disfavor. It was for many years the settled practice of Congress to grant the States upon the seaboard leave to lay duties at their ports for the improvement of the harbors, and itself to undertake the expense of no public works save those upon territory actually owned by the United States. But in later years the relaxation of presidential opposition and the admission of new States lying altogether away from the sea, and, therefore, quite unwilling to pay the tariffs which were building up the harbors of their eastern neighbors without any recompensing advantage to themselves who had no harbors, revived the plans which the vetoes of former times had rebuffed, and appropriations from the national coffers began freely to be made for the opening of the great water highways and the perfecting of the sea-gates of commerce. The inland States were silenced, because satisfied by a share in the benefits of national aid, which, being no longer indirect, was not confined to the sanctioning of state tariffs which none but the sea-board commonwealths could benefit by, but which consumers everywhere had to pay.

The greatest increase in appropriations of this class took place just after 1870. Since that date they have occupied a very prominent place in legislation, running from some twelve millions in the session of 1873-4 up and down through various figures to eighteen millions seven hundred thousand in the session of 1882-3, constituting during that decade the chief business of the Committee on Commerce, and finally having a special Standing Committee erected for their superintendence. They have thus culminated with the culmination of the protective tariff, and the so-called "American system" of protective tariffs and internal improvements has thus at last attained to its perfect work. The same prerogatives are accorded this new appropriations committee which have been secured to the greater Committee which deals with the estimates. Its reports may be made at any time when a member is not speaking, and stand in all respects upon the same footing as the bills proposing the annual grants. It is a special spending committee, with its own key to the Treasury.

But the Appropriation Committees of the two Houses, though, strictly speaking, the only committees of supply, have their work increased and supplemented by the numerous Committees which devote time and energy to creating demands upon the Treasury. There is a pension list in the estimates for whose payment the Committee on Appropriations has to provide every year; but the Committee on Pensions is constantly manufacturing new claims upon the public revenues.[5] There must be money forthcoming to build the new ships called for by the report of the Committee on Naval Affairs, and to meet the charges for the army equipment and reforms recommended by the Committee on Military Affairs. There are innumerable fingers in the budget pie.

It is principally in connection with appropriations that what has come to be known in our political slang as "log-rolling" takes place. Of course the chief scene of this sport is the private room of the Committee on Rivers and Harbors, and the season of its highest excitement, the hours spent in the passage of the River and Harbor Bill. "Log-rolling" is an exchange of favors. Representative A. is very anxious to secure a grant for the clearing of a small watercourse in his district, and representative B. is equally solicitous about his plans for bringing money into the hands of the contractors of his own constituency, whilst representative C. comes from a sea-port town whose modest harbor is neglected because of the treacherous bar across its mouth, and representative D. has been blamed for not bestirring himself more in the interest of schemes of improvement afoot amongst the enterprising citizens of his native place; so it is perfectly feasible for these gentlemen to put their heads together and confirm a mutual understanding that each will vote in Committee of the Whole for the grants desired by the others, in consideration of the promise that they will cry "aye" when his item comes on to be considered. It is not out of the question to gain the favoring ear of the reporting Committee, and a great deal of tinkering can be done with the bill after it has come into the hands of the House. Lobbying and log-rolling go hand in hand.

So much for estimates and appropriations. All questions of revenue are in their first stages in the hands of the House Committee of Ways and Means, and in their last, in charge of the Senate Committee on Finance. The name of the House Committee is evidently borrowed from the language of the British Parliament; the English Committee of Ways and Means is, however, the Commons itself sitting in Committee of the Whole to consider the statement and proposals of the Chancellor of the Exchequer, whilst ours is a Standing Committee of the House composed of eleven members, and charged with the preparation of all legislation relating to the raising of the revenue and to providing ways and means for the support of the government. We have, in English parliamentary phrase, put our Chancellorship of the Exchequer into commission. The chairman of the Committee figures as our minister of finance, but he really, of course, only represents the commission of eleven over which he presides.

All reports of the Treasury department are referred to this Committee of Ways and Means, which also, like the Committee on Appropriations, from time to time holds other more direct communications with the officers of revenue bureaux. The annual reports of the Secretary of the Treasury are generally quite full of minute information upon the points most immediately connected with the proper duties of the Committee. They are explicit with regard to the collection and disbursement of the revenues, with regard to the condition of the public debt, and with regard to the operation of all laws governing the financial policy of the departments. They are, in one aspect, the great yearly balance sheets, exhibiting the receipts and expenditures of the government, its liabilities and its credits; and, in another aspect, general views of the state of industry and of the financial machinery of the country, summarizing the information compiled by the bureau of statistics with reference to the condition of the manufactures and of domestic trade, as well as with regard to the plight of the currency and of the national banks. They are, of course, quite distinct from the "Letters" of the Secretary of the Treasury, which contain the estimates, and go, not to the Committee of Ways and Means, but to the Committee on Appropriations.

Though the duties of the Committee of Ways and Means in supervising the management of the revenues of the country are quite closely analogous to those of the British Chancellor of the Exchequer, the lines of policy in which they walk are very widely separated from those which he feels bound to follow. As I have said, the object which he holds constantly in view is to keep the annual balances as nearly as possible at an equilibrium. He plans to raise only just enough revenue to satisfy the grants made in Committee of Supply, and leave a modest surplus to cover possible errors in the estimates and probable fluctuations in the returns from taxation. Our Committee of Ways and Means, on the other hand, follow a very different policy. The revenues which they control are raised for a double object. They represent not only the income of the government, but also a carefully erected commercial policy to which the income of the government has for many years been incidental. They are intended to foster the manufactures of the country as well as to defray the expenses of federal administration. Were the maintenance of the government and the support of the public credit the chief objects of our national policy of taxation, it would undoubtedly be cast in a very different pattern. During a greater part of the lifetime of the present government, the principal feature of that policy has been a complex system of duties on imports, troublesome and expensive of collection, but nevertheless yielding, together with the license taxes of the internal revenue which later years have seen added to it, immense surpluses which no extravagances of the spending committees could exhaust. Duties few, small, and comparatively inexpensive of collection would afford abundant revenues for the efficient conduct of the government, besides comporting much more evidently with economy in financial administration. Of course, if vast revenues pour in over the barriers of an exacting and exorbitant tariff, amply sufficient revenues would flow in through the easy conduits of moderate and simple duties. The object of our financial policy, however, has not been to equalize receipts and expenditures, but to foster the industries of the country. The Committee of Ways and Means, therefore, do not concern themselves directly with regulating the income of the government—they know that that, in every probable event, will be more than sufficient—but with protecting the interests of the manufacturers as affected by the regulation of the tariff. The resources of the government are made incidental to the industrial investments of private citizens.

This evidently constitutes a very capital difference between the functions of the Chancellor of the Exchequer and those of our Committee of Ways and Means. In the policy of the former the support of the government is everything; with the latter the care of the industries of the country is the beginning and the end of duty. In the eyes of parliament enormous balances represent ignorant or improper management on the part of the ministers, and a succession of them is sure to cast a cabinet from office, to the lasting disgrace of the Chancellor of the Exchequer; but to the mind of Congress vast surpluses are indicative of nothing in particular. They indicate of course abundant returns from the duties, but the chief concern is, not whether the duties are fruitful, but whether they render the trades prosperous. Commercial interests are the essential consideration; excess of income is a matter of comparative indifference. The points of view characteristic of the two systems are thus quite opposite: the Committee of Ways and Means subordinates its housekeeping duties to its much wider extragovernmental business; the Chancellor of the Exchequer subordinates everything to economical administration.

This is evidently the meaning of the easy sovereignty, in the practice of the House, of questions of supply over questions of revenue. It is imperative to grant money for the support of the government, but questions of revenue revision may be postponed without inconvenience. The two things do not necessarily go hand in hand, as they do in the Commons. The reports of the Committee of Ways and Means are matters of quite as high privilege as the reports of the Committee on Appropriations, but they by no means stand an equal chance of gaining the consideration of the House and reaching a passage. They have no inseparable connection with the annual grants; the needed supplies will be forthcoming without any readjustments of taxation to meet the anticipated demands, because the taxes are not laid in the first instance with reference to the expenses which are to be paid out of their proceeds. If it were the function of the Committee of Ways and Means, as it is of the Chancellor of the Exchequer, to adjust the revenue to the expenditures, their reports would be as essential a part of the business of each session as are the reports of the Committee on Appropriations; but their proposals, occupying, as they do, a very different place in legislation, may go to the wall just as the proposals of the other Committees do at the demand of the chairman of the great spending Committee. The figures of the annual grants do not run near enough to the sum of the annual receipts to make them at all dependent on bills which concern the latter.

It would seem that the supervision exercised by Congress over expenditures is more thorough than that which is exercised by the Commons in England. In 1814 the House created a Standing Committee on Public Expenditures whose duty it should be "to examine into the state of the several public departments, and particularly into laws making appropriations of money, and to report whether the moneys have been disbursed conformably with such laws; and also to report from time to time such provisions and arrangements as may be necessary to add to the economy of the departments and the accountability of their officers"; but this Committee stood as the only committee of audit for but two years. It was not then abolished, but its jurisdiction was divided amongst six other Committees on Expenditures in the several departments, to which was added in 1860 a seventh, and in 1874 an eighth. There is thus a separate Committee for the audit of the accounts of each of the executive departments, beside which the original single Committee on Public Expenditures stands charged with such duties as may have been left it in the general distribution.[6] The duties of these eight Committees are specified with great minuteness in the rules. They are "to examine into the state of the accounts and expenditures respectively submitted to them, and to inquire and report particularly," whether the expenditures of the respective departments are warranted by law; "whether the claims from time to time satisfied and discharged by the respective departments are supported by sufficient vouchers, establishing their justness both as to their character and amount; whether such claims have been discharged out of funds appropriated therefor, and whether all moneys have been disbursed in conformity with appropriation laws; and whether any, or what, provisions are necessary to be adopted, to provide more perfectly for the proper application of the public moneys, and to secure the government from demands unjust in their character or extravagant in their amount." Besides exercising these functions of careful audit, they are, moreover, required to "report from time to time" any plans for retrenchment that may appear advisable in the interests of economy, or any measures that may be necessary to secure greater efficiency or to insure stricter accountability to Congress in the management of the departments; to ferret out all abuses that may make their appearance; and to see to it that no department has useless offices in its bureaux, or over or under-paid officers on its rolls.

But, though these Committees are so many and so completely armed with powers, indications are not wanting that more abuses run at large in the departments than they, with all their eyes, are able to detect. The Senate, though it has no similar permanent committees, has sometimes discovered dishonest dealings that had altogether escaped the vigilance of the eight House Committees; and even these eight occasionally, by a special effort, bring to light transactions which would never have been unearthed in the ordinary routine course of their usual procedure. It was a select committee of the Senate which, during the sessions of the Forty-seventh Congress, discovered that the "contingent fund" of the Treasury department had been spent in repairs on the Secretary's private residence, for expensive suppers spread before the Secretary's political friends, for lemonade for the delectation of the Secretary's private palate, for bouquets for the gratification of the Secretary's busiest allies, for carpets never delivered, "ice" never used, and services never rendered;[7] although these were secrets of which the honest faces of the vouchers submitted with the accounts gave not a hint.

It is hard to see how there could have been anything satisfactory or conclusive in the annual supervision of the public accounts during any but the latest years of this system of committee audit. Before 1870 our national book-keeping was much like that still in vogue in France. Credits once granted ran on without period until they were exhausted. There were always unexpended balances to confuse the accounts; and when the figures of the original grants had been on a too generous scale, as was often the case, these balances accumulated from year to year in immense surpluses, sometimes of many millions, of whose use no account was given, and which consequently afforded means for all sorts of extravagance and peculation. In 1870 this abuse was partially corrected by a law which limited such accumulations to a period of two years, and laid hands, on behalf of the Treasury, on the $174,000,-000 of unexpended balances which had by that time been amassed in the several departments; but it was not till 1874 that such a rule of expenditure and accounting was established as would make intelligent audit by the Committees possible, by a proper circumscription of the time during which credits could be drawn upon without a regrant.[8]

Such is a general view, in brief and without technical detail, of the chief features of our financial system, of the dealings of Congress with the questions of revenue, expenditure, and supply. The contrast which this system offers to the old-world systems, of which the British is the most advanced type, is obviously a very striking one. The one is the very opposite of the others. On the one hand is a financial policy regulated by a compact, coöperative ministry under the direction of a representative chamber, and on the other hand a financial policy directed by the representative body itself, with only clerical aid from the executive. In our practice, in other words, the Committees are the ministers, and the titular ministers only confidential clerks. There is no concurrence, not even a nominal alliance, between the several sections of this committee-ministry, though their several duties are clearly very nearly akin and as clearly mutually dependent. This feature of disintegration in leadership runs, as I have already pointed out, through all our legislation; but it is manifestly of much more serious consequence in financial administration than in the direction of other concerns of government. There can be no doubt that, if it were not for the fact that our revenues are not regulated with any immediate reference to the expenditures of the government, this method of spending according to the suggestions of one body, and taxing in obedience to the suggestions of another entirely distinct, would very quickly bring us into distress; it would unquestionably break down under any attempt to treat revenue and expenditure as mutually adjustable parts of a single, uniform, self-consistent system. They can be so treated only when they are under the management of a single body; only when all financial arrangements are based upon schemes prepared by a few men of trained minds and accordant principles, who can act with easy agreement and with perfect confidence in each other. When taxation is regarded only as a source of revenue and the chief object of financial management is the graduation of outlays by income, the credit and debit sides of the account must come under a single eye to be properly balanced; or, at the least, those officers who raise the money must see and be guided by the books of those who spend it.

It cannot, therefore, be reasonably regarded as matter of surprise that our financial policy has been without consistency or coherency, without progressive continuity. The only evidences of design to be discovered in it appear in those few elementary features which were impressed upon it in the first days of the government, when Congress depended upon such men as Hamilton and Gallatin for guidance in putting the finances into shape. As far as it has any invariable characteristics, or any traceable heredity, it is the handiwork of the sagacious men who first presided over the Treasury department. Since it has been altogether in the hands of congressional Committees it has so waywardly shifted from one rôle to another, and has with such erratic facility changed its principles of action and its modes of speech, to suit the temper and tastes of the times, that one who studies it hardly becomes acquainted with it in one decade before he finds that that was a season quite apart from and unlike both those which went before and those which succeeded. At almost every session Congress has made some effort, more or less determined, towards changing the revenue system in some essential portion; and that system has never escaped radical alteration for ten years together. Had revenue been graduated by the comparatively steady standard of the expenditures, it must have been kept stable and calculable; but depending, as it has done, on a much-debated and constantly fluctuating industrial policy, it has been regulated in accordance with a scheme which has passed through as many phases as there have been vicissitudes and vagaries in the fortunes of commerce and the tactics of parties.

This is the more remarkable because upon all fiscal questions Congress acts with considerable deliberation and care.

Financial legislation usually, if not always, occupies by far the most prominent place in the business of each session. Though other questions are often disposed of at odd moments, in haste and without thought, questions of revenue and supply are always given full measure of debate. The House of Representatives, under authority of the Rule before referred to, which enables it, as it were, to project the previous question into Committee of the Whole, by providing for the discharge of that Committee from the further consideration of any bill that is in its hands, or that may be about to be referred to it, after all amendments "pending and that may be offered" shall have been acted upon without debate, seldom hesitates, when any ordinary business is to be considered, to forbid to the proceedings of Committee of the Whole all freedom of discussion, and, consequently, almost all discretion as to the action to be taken; but this muzzle is seldom put upon the mouth of the Committee when appropriation or tariff bills are to be considered, unless the discussion in Committee wanders off into fields quite apart from the proper matter of the measure in hand, in which case the House interposes to check the irrelevant talk. Appropriation bills have, however, as I have shown, a much higher privilege than have bills affecting the tariff, and instances are not wanting in which the chairman of the Committee on Appropriations has managed to engross the time of the House in the disposal of measures prepared by his Committee, to the entire exclusion of any action whatever on important bills reported by the Committee of Ways and Means after the most careful and laborious deliberation. His prerogatives are never disputed in such a contest for consideration between a supply and a revenue bill, because these two subjects do not, under our system, necessarily go hand in hand. Ways and Means bills may and should be acted upon, but Supply bills must be.

It should be remarked in this connection, moreover, that much as Congress talks about fiscal questions, whenever permitted to do so by the selfish Appropriations Committee, its talk is very little heeded by the big world outside its halls. The noteworthy fact, to which I have already called attention, that even the most thorough debates in Congress fail to awaken any genuine or active interest in the minds of the people, has had its most striking illustrations in the course of our financial legislation; for, though the discussions which have taken place in Congress upon financial questions have been so frequent, so protracted, and so thorough, engrossing so large a part of the time of the House on their every recurrence, they seem, in almost every instance, to have made scarcely any impression at all upon the public mind. The Coinage Act of 1873, by which silver was demonetized, had been before the country many years, ere it reached adoption, having been time and again considered by Committees of Congress, time and again printed and discussed in one shape or another, and having finally gained acceptance apparently by sheer persistence and importunity. The Resumption Act of 1875, too, had had a like career of repeated considerations by Committees, repeated printings, and a full discussion by Congress; and yet when the "Bland Silver Bill" of 1878 was on its way through the mills of legislation, some of the most prominent newspapers of the country declared with confidence that the Resumption Act had been passed inconsiderately and in haste, almost secretly indeed; and several members of Congress had previously complained that the demonetization scheme of 1873 had been pushed surreptitiously through the courses of its passage, Congress having been tricked into accepting it, doing it scarcely knew what.

This indifference of the country to what is said in Congress, pointing, as it obviously does, to the fact that, though the Committees lead in legislation, they lead without concert or responsibility, and lead nobody in particular, that is, no compact and organized party force which can be made accountable for its policy, has also a further significance with regard to the opportunities and capacities of the constituencies. The doubt and confusion of thought which must necessarily exist in the minds of the vast majority of voters as to the best way of exerting their will in influencing the action of an assembly whose organization is so complex, whose acts are apparently so haphazard, and in which responsibility is spread so thin, throws constituencies into the hands of local politicians who are more visible and tangible than are the leaders of Congress, and generates, the while, a profound distrust of Congress as a body whose actions cannot be reckoned beforehand by any standard of promises made at elections or any programmes announced by conventions. Constituencies can watch and understand a few banded leaders who display plain purposes and act upon them with promptness; but they cannot watch or understand forty odd Standing Committees, each of which goes its own way in doing what it can without any special regard to the pledges of either of the parties from which its membership is drawn. In short, we lack in our political life the conditions most essential for the formation of an active and effective public opinion. "The characteristics of a nation capable of public opinion," says Mr. Bagehot, most sagacious of political critics, "is that . . . parties will be *organized;* in each there will be a leader, in each there will be some looked up to, and many who look up to them; the opinion of the party will be formed and suggested by the few, it will be criticised and accepted by the many." [9] And this is just the sort of party organization which we have not. Our parties have titular leaders at the polls in the persons of candidates, and nominal creeds in the resolutions of conventions, but no select few in whom to trust for guidance in the general policy of legislation, or to whom to look for suggestions of opinion. What man, what group of men, can speak for the Republican party or for the Democratic party? When our most conspicuous and influential politicians say anything about future legislation, no one supposes that they are speaking for their party, as those who have authority; they are known to speak only for themselves and their small immediate following of colleagues and friends.

The present relations between Congress and public opinion remind us of that time, in the reign of George III, when "the bulk of the English people found itself powerless to control the course of English government," when the government was divorced from "that general mass of national sentiment on which a government can alone safely ground itself." Then it was that English public opinion, "robbed as it was of all practical power, and thus stripped of the feeling of responsibility which the consciousness of power carries with it," "became ignorant and indifferent to the general progress of the age, but at the same time . . . hostile to Government because it was Government, disloyal to the Crown, averse from Parliament. For the first and last time . . . Parliament was unpopular, and its opponents secure of popularity." [10] Congress has in our own day become divorced from the "general mass of national sentiment," simply because there is no means by which the movements of that national sentiment can readily be registered in legislation. Going about as it does to please all sorts of Committees composed of all sorts of men, —the dull and the acute, the able and the cunning, the honest and the careless,—Congress evades judgment by avoiding all coherency of plan in its action. The constituencies can hardly tell whether the works of any particular Congress have been good or bad; at the opening of its sessions there was no determinate policy to look forward to, and at their close no accomplished plans to look back upon. During its brief lifetime both parties may have vacillated and gone astray, policies may have shifted and wandered, and untold mischief, together with some good, may have been done; but when all is reviewed, it is next to impossible oftentimes to distribute justly the blame and the praise. A few stubborn committee-men may be at the bottom of much of the harm that has been wrought, but they do not represent their party, and it cannot be clear to the voter how his ballot is to change the habits of Congress for the better. He distrusts Congress because he feels that he cannot control it.

The voter, moreover, feels that his want of confidence in Congress is justified by what he hears of the power of corrupt lobbyists to turn legislation to their own uses. He hears of enormous subsidies begged and obtained; of pensions procured on commission by professional pension solicitors; of appropriations made in the interest of dishonest contractors; and he is not altogether unwarranted in the conclusion that these are evils inherent in the very nature of Congress, for there can be no doubt that the power of the lobbyist consists in great part, if not altogether, in the facility afforded him by the Committee system. He must, in the natural course of things, have many most favorable opportunities for approaching the great money-dispensing Committees. It would be impracticable to work up his schemes in the broad field of the whole House, but in the membership of a Committee he finds manageable numbers. If he can gain the ear of the Committee, or of any influential portion of it, he has practically gained the ear of the House itself; if his plans once get footing in a committee report, they may escape criticism altogether, and it will, in any case, be very difficult to dislodge them. This accessibility of the Committees by outsiders gives to illegitimate influences easy approach at all points of legislation, but no Committees are affected by it so often or so unfortunately as are the Committees which control the public moneys. They are naturally the ones whose favor is oftenest and most importunately, as well as most insidiously, sought; and no description of our system of revenue, appropriation, and supply would be complete without mention of the manufacturers who cultivate the favor of the Committee of Ways and Means, of the interested persons who walk attendance upon the Committee on Rivers and Harbors, and of the mail-contractors and subsidy-seekers who court the Committee on Appropriations.

My last point of critical comment upon our system of financial administration I shall borrow from a perspicacious critic of congressional methods who recently wrote thus to one of the best of American journals: "So long as the debit side of the national account is managed by one set of men, and the credit side by another set, both sets working separately and in secret, without any public responsibility, and without any intervention on the part of the executive official who is nominally responsible; so long as these sets, being composed largely of new men every two years, give no attention to business except when Congress is in session, *and thus spend in preparing plans the whole time which ought to be spent in public discussion of plans already matured,* so that an immense budget is rushed through without discussion in a week or ten days,—just so long the finances will go from bad to worse, no matter by what name you call the party in power. No other nation on earth attempts such a thing, or could attempt it without soon coming to grief, our salvation thus far consisting in an enormous income, with practically no drain for military expenditure." [11] Unquestionably this strikes a very vital point of criticism. Congress spends its time working, in sections, at preparing plans, instead of confining itself to what is for a numerous assembly manifestly the much more useful and proper function of debating and revising plans prepared beforehand for its consideration by a commission of skilled men, old in political practice and in legislative habit, whose official life is apart from its own, though dependent upon its will. Here, in other words, is another finger pointing to Mr. Mill's question as to the best "legislative commission." Our Committees fall short of being the best form of commission, not only in being too numerous but also in being integral parts of the body which they lead, having no life apart from it. Probably the best working commission would be one which should make plans for government independently of the representative body, and in immediate contact with the practical affairs of administration, but which should in all cases look to that body for the sanctioning of those plans, and should be immediately responsible to it for their success when put into operation.

FOUR

This is a Senate, a Senate of equals, of men of individual honor and personal character, and of absolute independence. We know no masters, we acknowledge no dictators. This is a hall for mutual consultation and discussion, not an arena for the exhibition of champions.—DANIEL WEBSTER.

THE SENATE

The Senate of the United States has been both extravagantly praised and unreasonably disparaged, according to the predisposition and temper of its various critics. In the eyes of some it has a stateliness of character, an eminency of prerogative, and, for the most part, a wisdom of practice such as no other deliberative body possesses; whilst in the estimation of others it is now, whatever it may have been formerly, but a somewhat select company of leisurely "bosses," in whose companionship the few men of character and high purpose who gain admission to its membership find little that is encouraging and nothing that is congenial. Now of course neither of these extreme opinions so much as resembles the uncolored truth, nor can that truth be obtained by a judicious mixture of their milder ingredients. The truth is, in this case as in so many others, something quite commonplace and practical. The Senate is just what the mode of its election and the conditions of public life in this country make it. Its members are chosen from the ranks of active politicians, in accordance with a law of natural selection to which the state legislatures are commonly obedient; and it is probable that it contains, conse-

135

quently, the best men that our system calls into politics. If these best men are not good, it is because our system of government fails to attract better men by its prizes, not because the country affords or could afford no finer material.

It has been usual to suppose that the Senate was just what the Constitution intended it to be; that because its place in the federal system was exalted the aims and character of its members would naturally be found to be exalted as well; that because its term was long its foresight would be long also; or that because its election was not directly of the people demagogy would find no life possible in its halls. But the Senate is in fact, of course, nothing more than a part, though a considerable part, of the public service, and if the general conditions of that service be such as to starve statesmen and foster demagogues, the Senate itself will be full of the latter kind, simply because there are no others available. There cannot be a separate breed of public men reared specially for the Senate. It must be recruited from the lower branches of the representative system, of which it is only the topmost part. No stream can be purer than its sources. The Senate can have in it no better men than the best men of the House of Representatives; and if the House of Representatives attract to itself only inferior talent, the Senate must put up with the same sort. I think it safe to say, therefore, that, though it may not be as good as could be wished, the Senate is as good as it can be under the circumstances. It contains the most perfect product of our politics, whatever that product may be.

In order to understand and appreciate the Senate, therefore, one must know the conditions of public life in this country. What are those conditions? Well, in the first place, they are not what they were in the early years of the federal government; they are not what they were even twenty years ago; for in this, as in other things, the war between the States ends one distinct period and opens another. Between the great constructive statesmen of the revolutionary days and the reconstructing politicians of the sixties there came into public place and legislative influence a great race of constitutional lawyers. The questions which faced our statesmen while the Constitution was a-making were in the broadest sense questions of politics; but the questions which dominated our public life after the federal government had been successfully set up were questions of legal interpretation such as only lawyers could grapple with. All matters of policy, all doubts of legislation, even all difficulties of diplomacy, were measured by rules of constitutional construction. There was hardly a single affair of public concern which was not hung upon some peg of constitutional dogma in the testing-rooms of one or another of the contending schools of constitutional interpretation. Constitutional issues were ever the tides, questions of administrative policy seldom more than the eddies, of politics.

The Republicans under Jefferson drew their nourishment from constitutional belief no less than did the Federalists; the Whigs and Democrats of a later day lived on what was essentially the same diet, though it was served in slightly different forms; and the parties of to-day are themselves fain to go to these cooks of the olden time whenever they desire strong meat to fortify them against their present debility. The great questions attending the admission of new States to the Union and the annexation of foreign territory, as well as all the controversies which came in the train of the contest over slavery and the reserved powers of the States, were of the Constitution constitutional; and what other questions were then living— save those which found root in the great charter's implied powers, about which there was such constant noise of debate? It will be remembered that very few publicists opposed internal improvements, for instance, on the ground that they were unwise or uncalled for. No one who took a statesmanlike view of the matter could fail to see that the opening up of the great water-ways of the country, the construction of roads, the cutting of canals, or any public work which might facilitate inter-State commerce by making intercourse between the various portions of the Union easy and rapid, was sanctioned by every consideration of wisdom, as being in conformity with a policy at once national in its spirit and universal in its benefits. The doubt was, not as to what it would be best and most provident to do, but as to what it would be lawful to do; and the chief opponents of schemes of internal improvement based their dissent upon a careful meditation of the language of the

Constitution. Without its plain approval they would not move, even if they had to stand still all their days.

It was, too, with many professions of this spirit that the tariff was dealt with. It ran suddenly to the front as a militant party question in 1833, not as if a great free-trade movement had been set afoot which was to anticipate the mission of Cobden and Bright, but as an issue between federal taxation and the constitutional privileges of the States. The agricultural States were being, as they thought, very cruelly trodden down under the iron heel of that protectionist policy to whose enthronement they had themselves consented, and they fetched their hope of escape from the Constitution. The federal government unquestionably possessed, they admitted, and that by direct grant of the fundamental law, the right to impose duties on imports; but did that right carry with it the privilege of laying discriminating duties for other purposes than that of raising legitimate revenue? Could the Constitution have meant that South Carolina might be taxed to maintain the manufactures of New England?

Close upon the heels of the great tariff controversy of that time came the stupendous contest over the right of secession and the abolition of slavery; and again in this contest, as in all that had gone before, the party which was being hard driven sought refuge in the Constitution. This too was, in its first stages at least, a lawyer's question. It eventually slipped out of all lawyerly control, and was given over to be settled by the stern and savage processes of war; but it stayed with the constitutional lawyers as long as it could, and would have stayed with them to the end had it not itself been bigger than the Constitution and mixed with such interests and such passions as were beyond the control of legislatures or of law courts.

Such samples of the character which political questions have hitherto borne in this country are sufficient to remind all readers of our history of what have been the chief features of our politics, and may serve, without further elaboration, to illustrate the point I wish to emphasize. It is manifest how such a course of politics would affect statesmanship and political leadership. While questions affecting the proper con-

struction of the Constitution were the chief and most imperative questions pressing for settlement, great lawyers were in
demand; and great lawyers were, accordingly, forthcoming in
satisfaction of the demand. In a land like ours, where litigation
is facilitated by the establishment of many open and impartial
courts, great lawyers are a much more plentiful product than
great administrators, unless there be also some extraordinary
means for the encouragement of administrative talents. We
have, accordingly, always had plenty of excellent lawyers,
though we have often had to do without even tolerable administrators, and seem destined to endure the inconvenience
of hereafter doing without any constructive statesmen at all.
The constitutional issues of former times were so big and so
urgent that they brought great advocates into the field, despite
all the tendencies there were in our system towards depriving
leadership of all place of authority. In the presence of questions affecting the very structure and powers of the federal
government, parties had to rally with definite purpose and es-
pouse a distinct creed; and when the maintenance or over-
throw of slavery had ceased to be a question of constitutional
right, and had become a matter of contention between sentiment and vested rights,—between interest and passionate feeling,—there was of course a hot energy of contest between two
compact hosts and a quick elevation of forceful leaders.

The three stages of national growth which preceded the war
between the States were each of them creative of a distinct
class of political leaders. In the period of erection there were
great architects and master-builders; in the period of constitutional interpretation there were, at a distance from the people, great political schoolmen who pondered and expounded
the letter of the law, and, nearer the people, great constitutional advocates who cast the doctrines of the schoolmen into
policy; and in the period of abolitionist agitation there were
great masters of feeling and leaders of public purpose. The
publicists of the second period kept charge of the slavery
question, as I have said, as long as they could, and gave place
with bitter reluctance to the anti-slavery orators and pro-
slavery champions who were to talk the war-feeling into a
flame. But it was of course inevitable that the new movement

should have new leaders. It was essentially revolutionary in its tone and in its designs, and so quite out of the reach of those principles of action which had governed the policy of the older school of politicians. Its aim was to change, not to vindicate, the Constitution. Its leaders spoke, not words of counsel, but words of passion and of command. It was a crusade, not a campaign; the impetuous movement of a cause, not the canvass of a mooted measure. And, like every big, stirring cause, it had its leaders—leaders whose authority rested upon the affections and sympathies of the people rather than upon any attested wisdom or success of statesmanship. The war was the work, mediately, of philanthropists; and the reconstructions which followed the war were the hasty strokes of these same unbalanced knights of the crusade, full of bold feeling, but not of steady or far-sighted judgment.

The anti-slavery movement called forth leaders who, from the very nature of their calling, were more picturesque than any who had figured on the national stage since the notable play of the Revolution had gone off the boards; but it was no better cast in leading parts than had been the drama which immediately preceded it. When the constitution of a self-governing people is being consciously moulded by the rapid formation of precedent during the earliest periods of its existence, there are sure to be antagonistic beliefs, distinct and strong and active enough to take shape in the creeds of energetic parties, each led by the greatest advocates of its cherished principles. The season of our constitutional development, consequently, saw as fine a race of statesmen at the front of national affairs as have ever directed the civil policy of the country; and they, in turn, gave place to men brave to encounter the struggles of changed times, and fit to solve the doubts of a new set of events.

Since the war, however, we have come into a fourth period of national life, and are perplexed at finding ourselves denied a new order of statesmanship to suit the altered conditions of government. The period of federal construction is long passed; questions of constitutional interpretation are no longer regarded as of pressing urgency; the war has been fought, even the embers of its issues being now almost extinguished; and we are left to that unexciting but none the less capitally important business of every-day peaceful development and judicious administration to whose execution every nation in its middle age has to address itself with what sagacity, energy, and prudence it can command. It cannot be said that these new duties have as yet raised up any men eminently fit for their fulfillment. We have had no great administrators since the opening of this newest stage, and there is as yet no visible sign that any such will soon arise. The forms of government in this country have always been unfavorable to the easy elevation of talent to a station of paramount authority; and those forms in their present crystallization are more unfavorable than ever to the toleration of the leadership of the few, whilst the questions now most prominent in politics are not of such a nature as to compel skilled and trustworthy champions to come into the field, as did the constitutional issues and revolutionary agitations of other days. They are matters of a too quiet, business-like sort to enlist feeling or arouse enthusiasm.

It is, therefore, very unfortunate that only feeling or enthusiasm can create recognized leadership in our politics. There is no office set apart for the great party leader in our government. The powers of the Speakership of the House of Representatives are too cramped and covert; the privileges of the chairmanships of the chief Standing Committees are too limited in scope; the presidency is too silent and inactive, too little like a premiership and too much like a superintendency. If there be any one man to whom a whole party or a great national majority looks for guiding counsel, he must lead without office, as Daniel Webster did, or in spite of his office, as Jefferson and Jackson did. There must be something in the times or in the questions which are abroad to thrust great advocates or great masters of purpose into a non-official leadership, which is theirs because they represent in the greatest actions of their lives some principle at once vital and widely loved or hated, or because they possess in their unrivaled power of eloquent speech the ability to give voice to some such living theme. There must be a cause to be advanced which is greater than the trammels of governmental forms, and which, by authority of its own imperative voice, constitutes its advocates the leaders of the nation, though without giving them official title—without need of official title. No one is authorized to lead by reason of any official station known to our system. We call our real leaders by no names but their own: Mr. Webster was always Mr. Webster and never Prime Minister.

In a country which governs itself by means of a public meeting, a Congress or a Parliament, a country whose political life is representative, the only real leadership in governmental affairs must be legislative leadership—ascendency in the public meeting which decides everything. The leaders, if there be any, must be those who suggest the opinions and rule the actions of the representative body. We have in this country, therefore, no real leadership; because no man is allowed to direct the course of Congress, and there is no way of governing the country save through Congress, which is supreme. The chairman of a great Committee like the Committee of Ways and Means stands, indeed, at the sources of a very large and important stream of policy, and can turn that stream at his pleasure, or mix what he will with its waters; but there are whole provinces of policy in which he can have no authority at all. He neither directs, nor can often influence, those other chairmen who direct all the other important affairs of government. He, though the greatest of chairmen, and as great, it may be, as any other one man in the whole governmental system, is by no means at the head of the government. He is, as he feels every day, only a big wheel where there are many other wheels, some almost as big as he, and all driven, like himself, by fires which he does not kindle or tend.

In a word, we have no supreme executive ministry, like the great "Ministry of the Crown" over sea, in whose hands is the general management of legislation; and we have, consequently, no great prizes of leadership such as are calculated to stimulate men of strong talents to great and conspicuous public services. The Committee system is, as I have already pointed out, the very opposite of this. It makes all the prizes of leadership small, and nowhere gathers power into a few hands. It cannot be denied that this is in ordinary times, and in the absence of stirring themes, a great drawback, inasmuch as it makes legislative service unattractive to minds of the highest order, to whom the offer of really great place and power at the head of the governing assembly, the supreme council of the nation, would be of all things most attractive. If the presidency were competitive,—if it could be won by distinguished congressional service,—who can doubt that there would be a notable influx of talents into Congress and a significant elevation of tone and betterment of method in its proceedings; and yet the presidency is very far from being equal to a first-rate premiership.

There is, I know, one distinctive feature of legislative leadership which makes it seem to some not altogether to be desired; though it scarcely constitutes such an objection as to make no leadership at all seem preferable. It is the leadership of orators; it is the ascendancy of those who have a genius for talking. In the eyes of those who do not like it, it seems a leadership of artful dialecticians, the success of tricks of phrase, the victory of rushing declamation—government, not by the advice of statesman-like counselors, but by the wagging of ready tongues. Macaulay pointed out with his accustomed force of statement just the fact which haunts those who hold to such objections. The power of speaking, he said, which is so highly prized by politicians in a popular government, "may exist in the highest degree without judgment, without fortitude, without skill in reading the characters of men or the signs of the times, without any knowledge of the principles of legislation or of political economy, and without any skill in diplomacy or in the administration of war. Nay, it may well happen that those very intellectual qualities which give peculiar charm to the speeches of a public man may be incompatible with the qualities which would fit him to meet a pressing emergency with promptitude and firmness. It was thus with Charles Townshend. It was thus with Windham. It was a privilege to listen to those accomplished and ingenious orators. But in a perilous crisis they would be found inferior in all the qualities of rulers to such a man as Oliver Cromwell, who talked nonsense, or as William the Silent, who did not talk at all."

Nevertheless, it is to be observed that neither Windham nor

Townshend rose to places of highest confidence in the assembly which they served, and which they charmed by their attractive powers of speech; and that Cromwell would have been as unfit to rule anything but an autocratic commonwealth as would have been William the Silent to be anything but a Dutch governor. The people really had no voice in Cromwell's government. It was absolute. He would have been as much out of place in a representative government as a bull in a china shop. We would not have a Bismarck if we could.

Every species of government has the defects of its own qualities. Representative government is government by advocacy, by discussion, by persuasion, and a great, miscellaneous voting population is often misled by deceitful pleas and swayed by unwise counsels. But if one were to make a somewhat freer choice of examples than Macaulay permitted himself, it would be easy to multiply the instances of ruling orators of our race who have added to their gifts of eloquence conspicuous sagacity in the administration of affairs. At any rate, the men who have led popular assemblies have often been, like Hampden, rarely endowed with judgment, foresight, and steadfastness of purpose; like Walpole, amazingly quick in "reading the characters of men and the signs of the times"; like Chatham, masterful in ordering the conquests and the policies of the world; like Burke, learned in the profoundest principles of statecraft; like Canning, adroit in diplomacy; like Pitt, safe in times of revolution; like Peel, sagacious in finance; or, like Gladstone, skilled in every branch of political knowledge and equal to any strain of emergency.

It is natural that orators should be the leaders of a self-governing people. Men may be clever and engaging speakers, such as are to be found, doubtless, at half the bars of the country, without being equipped even tolerably for any of the high duties of the statesman; but men can scarcely be orators without that force of character, that readiness of resource, that clearness of vision, that grasp of intellect, that courage of conviction, that earnestness of purpose, and that instinct and capacity for leadership which are the eight horses that draw the triumphal chariot of every leader and ruler of free men. We could not object to being ruled again by such men as Henry and Otis and Samuel Adams; but they were products of revolution. They were inspired by the great causes of the time; and the government which they set up has left us without any ordinary, peaceful means of bringing men like them into public life. We should like to have more like them, but the violent exercise of revolution is too big a price to pay for them. Some less pungent diet is to be desired for the purpose of giving health to our legislative service. There ought to be some quiet, effective tonic, some mild stimulant, such as the certain prospect of winning highest and most honorable office, to infuse the best talent of the nation into our public life.

These, then, are the conditions of public life which make the House of Representatives what it is, a disintegrate mass of jarring elements, and the Senate what it is, a small, select, and leisurely House of Representatives. Or perhaps it would be nearer the whole truth to say that these are the circumstances and this the frame of government of which the two Houses form a part. Were the Senate not supplied principally by promotions from the House,—if it had, that is, a membership made up of men specially trained for its peculiar duties, —it would probably be much more effective than it is in fulfilling the great function of instructive and business-like debate of public questions; for its duties are enough unlike those of the House to be called peculiar. Men who have acquired all their habits in the matter of dealing with legislative measures in the House of Representatives, where committee work is everything and public discussion nothing but "talking to the country," find themselves still mere declaimers when they get into the Senate, where no previous question utters its interrupting voice from the tongues of tyrannical committee-men, and where, consequently, talk is free to all.[1] Only superior talents, such as very few men possess, could enable a Representative of long training to change his spots upon entering the Senate. Most men will not fit more than one sphere in life; and after they have been stretched or compressed to the measure of that one they will rattle about loosely or stick too tight in any other into which they may be thrust. Still, more or less adjustment takes place in every case. If a new Senator knock about too loosely amidst the free spaces of the rules of that august body, he will assuredly have some of his biggest corners knocked off and his angularities thus made smoother; if he stick fast amongst the dignified courtesies and punctilious observances of the upper chamber, he will, if he stick long enough, finally wear down to such a size, by jostling, as to attain some motion more or less satisfactory.

But it must be said, on the other hand, that even if the Senate were made up of something better than selections from the House, it would probably be able to do little more than it does in the way of giving efficiency to our system of legislation. For it has those same radical defects of organization which weaken the House. Its functions also, like those of the House, are segregated in the prerogatives of numerous Standing Committees.[2] In this regard Congress is all of a piece. There is in the Senate no more opportunity than exists in the House for gaining such recognized party leadership as would be likely to enlarge a man by giving him a sense of power, and to steady and sober him by filling him with a grave sense of responsibility. So far as its organization controls it, the Senate, notwithstanding the one or two special excellences which make it more temperate and often more rational than the House, has no virtue which marks it as of a different nature. Its proceedings bear most of the characteristic features of committee rule.[3] Its conclusions are suggested now by one set of its members, now by another set, and again by a third; an arrangement which is of course quite effective in its case, as in that of the House, in depriving it of that leadership which is valuable in more ways than in imparting distinct purpose to legislative action, because it concentrates party responsibility, attracts the best talents, and fixes public interest.

Some Senators are, indeed, seen to be of larger mental stature and built of stauncher moral stuff than their fellow-members, and it is not uncommon for individual members to become conspicuous figures in every great event in the Senate's deliberations. The public now and again picks out here and there a Senator who seems to act and to speak with true instinct of statesmanship and who unmistakably merits the confidence of colleagues and of people. But such a man, however eminent, is never more than *a* Senator. No one is *the* Senator. No one may speak for his party as well as for himself; no one exercises the special trust of acknowledged leadership. The Senate is merely a body of individual critics, representing most of the not very diversified types of a society substantially homogeneous; and the weight of every criticism uttered in its chamber depends upon the weight of the critic who utters it, deriving little if any addition to its specific gravity from connection with the designs of a purposeful party organization. I cannot insist too much upon this defect of congressional government, because it is evidently radical. Leadership with authority over a great ruling party is a prize to attract great competitors, and is in a free government the only prize that will attract great competitors. Its attractiveness is abundantly illustrated in the operations of the British system. In England, where members of the Cabinet, which is merely a Committee of the House of Commons, are the rulers of the empire, a career in the Commons is eagerly sought by men of the rarest gifts, because a career there is the best road, is indeed the only road, to membership of the great Committee. A part in the life of Congress, on the contrary, though the best career opened to men of ambition by our system, has no prize at its end greater than membership of some one of numerous Committees, between which there is some choice, to be sure, because some of them have great and others only small jurisdictions, but none of which has the distinction of supremacy in policy or of recognized authority to do more than suggest. And posts upon such Committees are the highest posts in the Senate just as they are in the House of Representatives.

In an address delivered on a recent occasion,[4] in the capacity of President of the Birmingham and Midland Institute, Mr. Froude, having in mind, of course, British forms of government, but looking mediately at all popular systems, said very pointedly that "In party government party life becomes like a court of justice. The people are the judges, the politicians the advocates, who," he adds caustically rather than justly, "only occasionally and by accident speak their real opinions." "The truly great political orators," he exclaims, "are the ornaments of mankind, the most finished examples of noble feeling and perfect expression, but they rarely understand the circumstances of their time. They feel passionately, but for that reason they cannot judge calmly." If we are to accept these judgments from Mr. Froude in the face of his reputation for thinking somewhat too independently of evidence, we should congratulate ourselves that we have in this country hit upon a system which, now that it has reached its perfection, has left little or no place for politicians to make false declarations or for the orator to coin fine expression for views which are only feelings, except outside of the legislative halls of the nation, upon the platform, where talk is all that is expected. It would seem as if the seer had a much more favorable opportunity in the committee-room than the orator can have, and with us it is the committee-room which governs the legislative chamber. The speech-making in the latter neither makes nor often seriously affects the plans framed in the former; because the plans are made before the speeches are uttered. This is self-evident of the debates of the House; but even the speeches made in the Senate, free, full, and earnest as they seem, are made, so to speak, after the fact—not to determine the actions but to air the opinions of the body.

Still, it must be regarded as no inconsiderable addition to the usefulness of the Senate that it enjoys a much greater freedom of discussion than the House can allow itself. It permits itself a good deal of talk in public about what it is doing,[5] and it commonly talks a great deal of sense. It is small enough to make it safe to allow individual freedom to its members, and to have, at the same time, such order and sense of proportion in its proceedings as is characteristic of small bodies, like boards of college trustees or of commercial directors, who feel that their main object is business, not speech-making, and so say all that is necessary without being tedious, and do what they are called upon to do without need of driving themselves with hurrying rules. Such rules, they seem to feel, are meant only for big assemblies which have no power of self-control. Of course the Senate talks more than an average board of directors would, because the corporations which it represents are States, made up, politically speaking, of numerous popular constituencies to which Senators, no less than Representatives, must make speeches of a sort which, considering their fellow-members alone, would be unnecessary if not impertinent and out of taste, in the Senate chamber, but which will sound best in the ears of the people, for whose ears they are intended, if delivered there. Speeches which, so to say, run in the name of the Senate's business will generally be more effectual for campaign uses at home than any speech could be which should run in the name of the proper topics of the stump. There is an air of doing one's duty by one's party in speaking party platitudes or uttering party defiances on the floor of the Senate or of the House.

Of course, however, there is less temptation to such speech-making in the Senate than in the House. The House knows the terrible possibilities of this sort in store for it, were it to give perfect freedom of debate to its three hundred and twenty-five members, in these days when frequent mails and tireless tongues of telegraphy bring every constituency within easy earshot of Washington; and it therefore seeks to confine what little discussion it indulges in to the few committee-men specially in charge of the business of each moment. But the Senate is small and of settled habits, and has no such bugbear to trouble it. It can afford to do without any *clôture* or previous question. No Senator is likely to want to speak on all the topics of the session, or to prepare more speeches than can conveniently be spoken before adjournment is imperatively at hand. The House can be counted upon to waste enough time to leave some leisure to the upper chamber.

And there can be no question that the debates which take place every session in the Senate are of a very high order of excellence. The average of the ability displayed in its discussions not infrequently rises quite to the level of those controversies of the past which we are wont to call great because they furnished occasion to men like Webster and Calhoun and Clay, whom we cannot now quite match in mastery of knowledge and of eloquence. If the debates of the present are smothered amongst the innumerable folios of the "Record," it is not because they do not contain utterances worthy to be heeded and to gain currency, but because they do not deal with questions of passion or of national existence, such as ran

through all the earlier debates, or because our system so ob-
scures and complicates party rule in legislation as to leave
nothing very interesting to the public eye dependent upon the
discussions of either House or Senate. What that is picturesque,
or what that is vital in the esteem of the partisan, is there in
these wordy contests about contemplated legislation? How
does anybody know that either party's prospects will be much
affected by what is said when Senators are debating, or, for
that matter, by what is voted after their longest flights of
controversy?

Still, though not much heeded, the debates of the Senate are
of great value in scrutinizing and sifting matters which come
up from the House. The Senate's opportunities for open and
unrestricted discussion and its simple, comparatively unencum-
bered forms of procedure, unquestionably enable it to fulfill
with very considerable success its high functions as a chamber
of revision.

When this has been claimed and admitted, however, it still
remains to be considered whether two chambers of equal
power strengthen by steadying, or weaken by complicating, a
system of representative government like our own. The utility
and excellence of a bicameral system has never, I believe, been
seriously questioned in this country; but M. Turgot smiles with
something like contempt at our affectation in copying the
House of Lords without having any lords to use for the purpose; and in our own day Mr. Bagehot, who is much more
competent to speak on this head than was M. Turgot, has
avowed very grave doubts as to the practical advantage of a
two-headed legislature—each head having its own independent
will. He finds much to recommend the House of Lords in the
fact that it is not, as theory would have it, coördinate and
coequal with the House of Commons, but merely "a revising
and suspending House," altering what the Commons have
done hastily or carelessly, and sometimes rejecting "Bills on
which the House of Commons is not yet thoroughly in earnest,
—upon which the nation is not yet determined." [6] He points
out the fact that the House of Lords has never in modern
times been, as a House, coequal in power with the House of
Commons. Before the Reform Bill of 1832 the peers were all-

powerful in legislation; not, however, because they were members of the House of Lords, but because they nominated most of the members of the House of Commons. Since that disturbing reform they have been thrown back upon the functions in which they never were strong, the functions of a deliberative assembly. These are the facts which seem to Mr. Bagehot to have made it possible for legislation to make easy and satisfactory progress under a system whose theory provided for fatal dead-locks between the two branches of the supreme legislature.

In his view "the evil of two coequal Houses of distinct natures is obvious." "Most constitutions," he declares, "have committed this blunder. The two most remarkable Republican institutions in the world commit it. In both the American and Swiss Constitutions the Upper House has as much authority as the second; it could produce the maximum of impediment—a dead-lock, if it liked; if it does not do so, it is owing not to the goodness of the legal constitution, but to the discreetness of the members of the Chamber. In both these constitutions this dangerous division is defended by a peculiar doctrine. . . . It is said that there must be in a federal government some institution, some authority, some body possessing a veto in which the separate States comprising the Confederation are all equal. I confess this doctrine has to me no self-evidence, and it is assumed, but not proved. The State of Delaware is not equal in power or influence to the State of New York, and you cannot make it so by giving it an equal veto in an Upper Chamber. The history of such an institution is indeed most natural. A little State will like, and must like, to see some token, some memorial mark, of its old independence preserved in the Constitution by which that independence is extinguished. But it is one thing for an institution to be natural, and another for it to be expedient. If indeed it be that a federal government compels the erection of an Upper Chamber of conclusive and coördinate authority, it is one more in addition to the many other inherent defects of that kind of government. It may be necessary to have the blemish, but it is a blemish just as much."

It would be in the highest degree indiscreet to differ lightly with any conclusion to which Mr. Bagehot may have come in viewing that field of critical exposition in which he was supreme, the philosophical analysis, namely, of the English Constitution; and it must be apparent to any one who reads the passage I have just now quoted that his eye sees very keenly and truly even when he looks across sea at institutions which were repugnant to his own way of thinking. But it is safe to say that he did not see all in this instance, and that he was consequently in error concerning the true nature of our federal legislative system. His error, nevertheless, appears, not when we look only at the facts which he held up to view, but when we look at other facts which he ignored. It is true that the existence of two coequal Houses is an evil when those two Houses are of distinct natures, as was the case under the Victorian Constitution to which Mr. Bagehot refers by way of illustrative example. Under that Constitution all legislative business was sometimes to be seen quite suspended because of irreconcilable differences of opinion between the Upper House, which represented the rich wool-growers of the colony, and the Lower Assembly, which represented the lesser wool-growers, perhaps, and the people who were not wool-growers at all. The Upper House, in other words, was a class chamber, and thus stood quite apart from anything like the principle embodied in our own Senate, which is no more a class chamber than is the House of Representatives.

The prerogatives of the Senate do, indeed, render our legislative system more complex, and for that reason possibly more cumbersome, than the British; for our Senate can do more than the House of Lords. It can not only question and stay the judgment of the Commons, but may always with perfect safety act upon its own judgment and gainsay the more popular chamber to the end of the longest chapter of the bitterest controversy. It is quite as free to act as is any other branch of the government, and quite as sure to have its acts regarded. But there is safety and ease in the fact that the Senate never wishes to carry its resistance to the House to that point at which resistance must stay all progress in legislation; because there is really a "latent unity" between the

Senate and the House which makes continued antagonism between them next to impossible—certainly in the highest degree improbable. The Senate and the House are of different origins, but virtually of the same nature. The Senate is less democratic than the House, and consequently less sensible to transient phases of public opinion; but it is no less sensible than the House of its ultimate accountability to the people, and is consequently quite as obedient to the more permanent and imperative judgments of the public mind. It cannot be carried so quickly by every new sentiment, but it can be carried quickly enough. There is a main chance of election time for it as well as for the House to think about.

By the mode of its election and the greater length of the term by which its seats are held, the Senate is almost altogether removed from that temptation to servile obedience to the whims of popular constituencies to which the House is constantly subject, without as much courage as the Senate has to guard its virtue. But the men who compose the Senate are of the same sort as the members of the House of Representatives, and represent quite as various classes. Nowadays many of the Senators are, indeed, very rich men, and there has come to be a great deal of talk about their vast wealth and the supposed aristocratic tendencies which it is imagined to breed. But even the rich Senators cannot be said to be representatives of a class, as if they were all opulent wool-growers or great land-owners. Their wealth is in all sorts of stocks, in all sorts of machinery, in all sorts of buildings, in possessions of all the sorts possible in a land of bustling commerce and money-making industries. They have made their money in a hundred different ways, or have inherited it from fathers who amassed it in enterprises too numerous to imagine; and they have it invested here, there, and everywhere, in this, that, and everything. Their wealth represents no class interests, but all the interests of the commercial world. It represents the majority of the nation, in a word; and so they can probably be trusted not to neglect one set of interests for another; not to despoil the trader for the sake of the farmer, or the farmer for the sake of the wool-grower, or the wool-grower for the behoof of the herder of short-horned cattle. At least the Senate is quite as trustworthy in this regard as is the House of Representatives.

Inasmuch as the Senate is thus separated from class interests and quite as representative of the nation at large as is the House of Representatives, the fact that it is less quickly sensitive to the hasty or impulsive movements of public opinion constitutes its value as a check, a steadying weight, in our very democratic system. Our English cousins have worked out for themselves a wonderfully perfect scheme of government by gradually making their monarchy unmonarchical. They have made of it a republic steadied by a reverenced aristocracy and pivoted upon a stable throne. And just as the English system is a limited monarchy because of Commons and Cabinet, ours may be said to be a limited democracy because of the Senate. This has in the trial of the scheme proved the chief value of that upper chamber which was instituted principally as an earnest of the abiding equality and sovereignty of the States. At any rate, this is the most conspicuous, and will prove to be the most lasting, use of the Senate in our system. It is valuable in our democracy in proportion as it is undemocratic. I think that a philosophical analysis of any successful and beneficent system of self-government will disclose the fact that its only effectual checks consist in a mixture of elements, in a combination of seemingly contradictory political principles; that the British government is perfect in proportion as it is unmonarchical, and ours safe in proportion as it is undemocratic; that the Senate saves us often from headlong popular tyranny.

"The value, spirit, and essence of the House of Commons," said Burke, "consists in its being the express image of the feelings of the nation"; but the image of the nation's feelings should not be the only thing reflected by the constitution of a free government. It is indispensable that, besides the House of Representatives which runs on all fours with popular sentiment, we should have a body like the Senate which may refuse to run with it at all when it seems to be wrong—a body which has time and security enough to keep its head, if only now and then and but for a little while, till other people have had time to think. The Senate is fitted to do deliberately and well the revising which is its properest function, because its position as a representative of state sovereignty is one of eminent dignity, securing for it ready and sincere respect, and because popular demands, ere they reach it with definite and authoritative suggestion, are diluted by passage through the feelings and conclusions of the state legislatures, which are the Senate's only immediate constituents. The Senate commonly feels with the House, but it does not, so to say, feel so fast. It at least has a chance to be the express image of those judgments of the nation which are slower and more temperate than its feelings.

This it is which makes the Senate "the most powerful and efficient second chamber that exists," [7] and this it is which constitutes its functions one of the effectual checks, one of the real balances, of our system; though it is made to seem very insignificant in the literary theory of the Constitution, where the checks of state upon federal authorities, of executive prerogatives upon legislative powers, and of Judiciary upon President and Congress, though some of them in reality inoperative from the first and all of them weakened by many "ifs" and "buts," are made to figure in the leading rôles, as the characteristic Virtues, triumphing over the characteristic Vices, of our new and original political Morality-play.

It should, however, be accounted a deduction from the Senate's usefulness that it is seldom sure of more than two thirds of itself for more than four years at a time. In order that its life may be perpetual, one third of its membership is renewed or changed every two years, each third taking its turn at change or renewal in regular succession; and this device has, of course, an appreciably weakening effect on the legislative sinews of the Senate. Because the Senate mixes the parties in the composition of its Committees just as the House does, and those Committees must, consequently, be subjected to modification whenever the biennial senatorial elections bring in new men, freshly promoted from the House or from gubernatorial chairs. Places must be found for them at once in the working organization which busies itself in the committee-rooms. Six years is not the term of the Senate, but only of each Senator.

Reckoning from any year in which one third of the Senate is elected, the term of the majority,—the two thirds not affected by the election,—is an average of the four and the two years which it has to live. There is never a time at which two thirds of the Senate have more than four years of appointed service before them. And this constant liability to change must, of course, materially affect the policy of the body. The time assured it in which to carry out any enterprise of policy upon which it may embark is seldom more than two years, the term of the House. It may be checked no less effectually than the lower House by the biennial elections, albeit the changes brought about in its membership are effected, not directly by the people, but indirectly and more slowly by the mediate operation of public opinion through the legislatures of the States.

In estimating the value of the Senate, therefore, as a branch of the national legislature, we should offset the committee organization, with its denial of leadership which disintegrates the Senate, and that liability to the biennial infusion of new elements which may at any time interrupt the policy and break the purpose of the Senate, against those habits of free and open debate which clear its mind, and to some extent the mind of the public, with regard to the nation's business, doing much towards making legislation definite and consistent, and against those great additions to its efficiency which spring from its observation of "slow and steady forms" of procedure, from the mediate election which gives it independence, and from its having a rational and august cause for existing.

When we turn to consider the Senate in its relations with the executive, we see it no longer as a legislative chamber, but as a consultative executive council. And just here there is to be noted an interesting difference between the relations of the Senate with the President and its relations with the departments, which are in constitutional theory one with the President. It deals directly with the President in acting upon nominations and upon treaties. It goes into "executive session" to handle without gloves the acts of the chief magistrate. Its dealings with the departments, on the other hand, are, like those of the House, only indirect. Its legislative, not its executive, function is the whip which coerces the Secretaries. Its will is the supreme law in the offices of the government; and yet it orders policy by no direct word to the departments. It does not consult and negotiate with them as it does with the President, their titular head. Its immediate agents, the Committees, are not the recognized constitutional superiors of Secretary A. or Comptroller B.; but these officials cannot move a finger or plan more than a paltry detail without looking to it that they render strict obedience to the wishes of these outside, uncommissioned, and irresponsible, but none the less authoritative and imperative masters.

This feature of the Senate's power over the executive does not, however, call for special emphasis here, because it is not a power peculiar to the Senate, this overlordship of the departments, but one which it possesses in common with the House of Representatives,—simply an innate and inseparable part of the absolutism of a supreme legislature. It is the Senate's position as the President's council in some great and many small matters which call for particular discussion. Its general tyranny over the departments belongs rather with what I am to say presently when looking at congressional government from the stand-point of the executive.

The greatest consultative privilege of the Senate,—the greatest in dignity, at least, if not in effect upon the interests of the country,—is its right to a ruling voice in the ratification of treaties with foreign powers. I have already alluded to this privilege, for the purpose of showing what weight it has had in many instances in disarranging the ideal balance supposed to exist between the powers of Congress and the constitutional prerogatives of the President; but I did not then stop to discuss the organic reasons which have made it impossible that there should be any real consultation between the President and the Senate upon such business, and which have, consequently, made disagreement and even antagonism between them probable outcomes of the system. I do not consult the auditor who scrutinizes my accounts when I submit to him my books, my vouchers, and a written report of the business I have negotiated. I do not take his advice and seek his consent; I simply ask his endorsement or invite his condemnation.

I do not sue for his coöperation, but challenge his criticism. And the analogy between my relations with the auditor and the relations of the President with the Senate is by no means remote. The President really has no voice at all in the conclusions of the Senate with reference to his diplomatic transactions, or with reference to any of the matters upon which he consults it; and yet without a voice in the conclusion there is no consultation. Argument and an unobstructed interchange of views upon a ground of absolute equality are essential parts of the substance of genuine consultation. The Senate, when it closes its doors, upon going into "executive session," closes them upon the President as much as upon the rest of the world. He cannot meet their objections to his courses except through the clogged and inadequate channels of a written message or through the friendly but unauthoritative offices of some Senator who may volunteer his active support. Nay, in many cases the President may not even know what the Senate's objections were. He is made to approach that body as a servant conferring with his master, and of course deferring to that master. His only power of compelling compliance on the part of the Senate lies in his initiative in negotiation, which affords him a chance to get the country into such scrapes, so pledged in the view of the world to certain courses of action, that the Senate hesitates to bring about the appearance of dishonor which would follow its refusal to ratify the rash promises or to support the indiscreet threats of the Department of State.

The machinery of consultation between the Senate and the President is of course the committee machinery. The Senate sends treaties to its Standing Committee on Foreign Relations, which ponders the President's messages accompanying the treaties and sets itself to understand the situation in the light of all the information available. If the President wishes some more satisfactory mode of communication with the Senate than formal message-writing, his only door of approach is this Committee on Foreign Relations. The Secretary of State may confer with its chairman or with its more influential members. But such a mode of conference is manifestly much less than a voice in the deliberations of the Senate itself,—much less than meeting that body face to face in free consultation and equal debate. It is almost as distinctly dealing with a foreign power as were the negotiations preceding the proposed treaty. It must predispose the Senate to the temper of an overseer.[8]

Still, treaties are not every-day affairs with us, and exceptional business may create in Senators an exceptional sense of responsibility, and dispose them to an unwonted desire to be dispassionate and fair. The ratification of treaties is a much more serious matter than the consideration of nominations which every session constitutes so constant a diversion from the more ponderous business of legislation. It is in dealing with nominations, however, that there is the most friction in the contact between the President and his overlord, the Senate. One of the most noteworthy instances of the improper tactics which may arise out of these relations was the case of that Mr. Smythe, at the time Collector for the port of New York, whom, in 1869, President Grant nominated Minister to the Court of St. Petersburg. The nomination, as looking towards an appointment to diplomatic service, was referred to the Committee on Foreign Relations, of which Mr. Charles Sumner was then chairman. That Committee rejected the nomination; but Smythe had great influence at his back and was himself skilled beyond most men in the arts of the lobby. He accordingly succeeded in securing such support in the Senate as to become a very formidable dog in the manger, not himself gaining the appointment, but for a time blocking all other appointments and bringing the business of the Senate altogether to a standstill, because he could not.[9] Smythe himself is forgotten; but no observer of the actual conditions of senatorial power can fail to see the grave import of the lesson which his case teaches, because his case was by no means an isolated one. There have been scores of others quite as bad; and we could have no assurance that there might not in the future be hundreds more, had not recent movements in the direction of a radical reform of the civil service begun to make nominations represent, not the personal preference of the President or the intrigues of other people, but honest, demonstrated worth, which the Senate is likely to feel forced to accept without question, when the reform reaches the highest grades of the service.

In discussing the Senate's connection with the civil service and the abuses surrounding that connection, one is, therefore, discussing a phase of congressional government which promises soon to become obsolete. A consummation devoutly to be wished!—and yet sure when it comes to rob our politics of a feature very conspicuous and very characteristic, and in a sense very entertaining. There are not many things in the proceedings of Congress which the people care to observe with any diligence, and it must be confessed that scandalous transactions in the Senate with reference to nominations were among the few things that the country watched and talked about with keen relish and interest. This was the personal element which always had spice in it. When Senator Conkling resigned in a huff because he could not have whom he liked in the collectorship of the port of New York, the country rubbed its hands; and when the same imperious politician sought reëlection as a vindication of that unconstitutional control of nominations which masqueraded as "the courtesy of the Senate," the country discussed his chances with real zest and chuckled over the whole affair in genuine glee. It was a big fight worth seeing. It would have been too bad to miss it.

Before the sentiment of reform had become strong enough to check it, this abuse of the consultative privileges of the Senate in the matter of nominations had assumed such proportions as to seem to some the ugliest deformity in our politics. It looked as if it were becoming at once the weakest and the most tried and strained joint of our federal system. If there was to be a break, would it not be there, where was the severest wear and tear? The evil practices seemed the more ineradicable because they had arisen in the most natural manner. The President was compelled, as in the case of treaties, to obtain the sanction of the Senate without being allowed any chance of consultation with it; and there soon grew up within the privacy of "executive session" an understanding that the wishes and opinions of each Senator who was of the President's own party should have more weight than even the inclinations of the majority in deciding upon the fitness or desirability of persons proposed to be appointed to offices in that Senator's State. There was the requisite privacy to shield from public condemnation the practice arising out of such an understanding; and the President himself was always quite out of earshot, hearing only of results, of final votes.

All through the direct dealings of the Senate with the President there runs this characteristic spirit of irresponsible dictation. The President may tire the Senate by dogged persistence, but he can never deal with it upon a ground of real equality. He has no real presence in the Senate. His power does not extend beyond the most general suggestion. The Senate always has the last word. No one would desire to see the President possessed of authority to overrule the decisions of the Senate, to treat with foreign powers, and appoint thousands of public officers, without any other than that shadowy responsibility which he owes to the people that elected him; but it is certainly an unfortunate feature of our government that Congress governs without being put into confidential relations with the agents through whom it governs. It dictates to another branch of the government which was intended to be coördinate and coequal with it, and over which it has no legalized authority as of a master, but only the authority of a bigger stockholder, of a monopolist indeed, of all the energetic prerogatives of the government. It is as if the Army and Navy Departments were to be made coördinate and coequal, but the absolute possession and control of all ammunition and other stores of war given to the one and denied the other. The executive is taken into partnership with the legislature upon a salary which may be withheld, and is allowed no voice in the management of the business. It is simply charged with the superintendence of the employees.

It was not essentially different in the early days when the President in person read his message to the Senate and the House together as an address, and the Senate in a body carried its reply to the executive mansion. The address was the formal communication of an outsider just as much as the message of to-day is, and the reply of the Senate was no less a formal document which it turned aside from its regular business to prepare. That meeting face to face was not consultation. The English Parliament does not consult with the sovereign when it assembles to hear the address from the throne.

It would, doubtless, be considered quite improper to omit from an essay on the Senate all mention of the Senate's President; and yet there is very little to be said about the Vice-President of the United States. His position is one of anomalous insignificance and curious uncertainty. Apparently he is not, strictly speaking, a part of the legislature,—he is clearly not a member,—yet neither is he an officer of the executive. It is one of the remarkable things about him, that it is hard to find in sketching the government any proper place to discuss him. He comes in most naturally along with the Senate to which he is tacked; but he does not come in there for any great consideration. He is simply a judicial officer set to moderate the proceedings of an assembly whose rules he has had no voice in framing and can have no voice in changing. His official stature is not to be compared with that of the Speaker of the House of Representatives. So long as he is Vice-President, he is inseparable officially from the Senate; his importance consists in the fact that he may cease to be Vice-President. His chief dignity, next to presiding over the Senate, lies in the circumstance that he is awaiting the death or disability of the President. And the chief embarrassment in discussing his office is, that in explaining how little there is to be said about it one has evidently said all there is to say.

FIVE

Every political constitution in which different bodies share the supreme power is only enabled to exist by the forbearance of those among whom this power is distributed.—LORD JOHN RUSSELL.

Simplicity and logical neatness are not the good to be aimed at in politics, but freedom and order, with props against the pressure of time, and arbitrary will, and sudden crises.—THEO. WOOLSEY.

Nothing, indeed, will appear more certain, on any tolerable consideration of this matter, than that every sort of government ought to have its administration correspondent to its legislature.—BURKE.

THE EXECUTIVE

It is at once curious and instructive to note how we have been forced into practically amending the Constitution without constitutionally amending it. The legal processes of constitutional change are so slow and cumbersome that we have been constrained to adopt a serviceable framework of fictions which enables us easily to preserve the forms without laboriously obeying the spirit of the Constitution, which will stretch as the nation grows. It would seem that no impulse short of the impulse of self-preservation, no force less than the force of revolution, can nowadays be expected to move the cumbrous machinery of formal amendment erected in Article Five. That must be a tremendous movement of opinion which can sway two thirds of each House of Congress and the people of three fourths of the States. Mr. Bagehot has pointed out that one consequence of the existence of this next to immovable machinery "is that the most obvious evils cannot be quickly remedied," and "that a clumsy working and a curious technicality mark the politics of a rough-and-ready people. The practical arguments and legal disquisitions in America," continues he, "are often like those of trustees carrying out a misdrawn will,—the sense of what they mean is good, but it can never be worked out fully or defended simply, so hampered is it by the old words of an old testament." [1] But much the greater consequence is that we have resorted, almost unconscious of the political significance of what we did, to extra-constitutional means of modifying the federal system where it has proved to be too refined by balances of divided authority to suit practical uses,—to be out of square with the main principle of its foundation, namely, government by the people through their representatives in Congress.

Our method of choosing Presidents is a notable illustration of these remarks. The difference between the actual and the constitutional modes is the difference between an ideal nonpartisan choice and a choice made under party whips; the difference between a choice made by independent, unpledged electors acting apart in the States and a choice made by a national party convention. Our Executive, no less than the English and French Executives, is selected by a representative, deliberative body, though in England and France the election is controlled by a permanent legislative chamber, and here by a transient assembly chosen for the purpose and dying with the execution of that purpose. In England the whole cabinet is practically elective. The French Chambers formally elect the President, the titular head of the government, and the President regards only the will of the Assembly in appointing the Prime Minister, who is the energetic head of the government, and who, in his turn, surrounds himself with colleagues who have the confidence of the legislature. And the French have but copied the English constitution, which makes the executive Ministry the representatives of the party majority in the Commons. With us, on the other hand, the President is elected by one representative body, which has nothing to do with him after his election, and the cabinet must be approved by another representative body, which has nothing directly to do with them after their appointment.

Of course I do not mean that the choice of a national convention is literally election. The convention only nominates a candidate. But that candidate is the only man for whom the electors of his party can vote; and so the expression of the preference of the convention of the dominant party is practically equivalent to election, and might as well be called election by any one who is writing of broad facts, and not of fine distinctions. The sovereign in England picks out the man who is to be Prime Minister, but he must pick where the Commons point; and so it is simpler, as well as perfectly true, to say that the Commons elect the Prime Minister. My agent does not select the particular horse I instruct him to buy. This is just the plain fact,—that the electors are the agents of the national conventions; and this fact constitutes more than an amendment of that original plan which would have had all the electors to be what the first electors actually were, trustworthy men given *carte blanche* to vote for whom they pleased, casting their ballots in thirteen state capitals in the hope that they would happen upon a majority agreement.

It is worth while, too, to notice another peculiarity of this elective system. There is a thorough-going minority representation in the assemblies which govern our elections. Across the ocean a Liberal Prime Minister is selected by the representatives only of those Liberals who live in Liberal constituencies; those who live elsewhere in a helpless minority, in a Conservative district, having of course no voice in the selection. A Conservative Premier, in like manner, owes nothing to those Conservatives who were unable to return a member to Parliament. So far as he is concerned, they count for Liberals, since their representative in the Commons is a Liberal. The parliaments which select our Presidents, on the contrary, are, each of them, all of a kind. No state district can have so few Republicans in it as not to be entitled to a representative in the national Republican convention equal to that of the most unanimously Republican district in the country; and a Republican State is accorded as full a representation in a Democratic convention as is the most Democratic of her sister States.

We had to pass through several stages of development before the present system of election by convention was reached. At the first two presidential elections the electors were left free to vote as their consciences and the Constitution bade them; for the Constitution bade them vote as they deemed best, and it did not require much discretion to vote for General Washington. But when General Washington was out of the race, and new parties began to dispute the field with the Federalists, party managers could not help feeling anxious about the votes of the electors, and some of those named to choose the second President were, accordingly, pledged beforehand to vote thus and so. After the third presidential election there began to be congressional oversight of the matter. From 1800 to 1824 there was an unbroken succession of caucuses of the Republican members of Congress to direct the action of the party electors; and nomination by caucus died only when the Republican party became virtually the only party worth reckoning with,—the only party for whom nomination was worth while,—and then public opinion began to cry out against such secret direction of the monopoly. In 1796 the Federalist congressmen had held an informal caucus to ascertain their minds as to the approaching election; but after that they refrained from further experiment in the same direction, and contented themselves with now and then a sort of convention until they had no party to convene. In 1828 there was a sort of dropping fire of nominations from state legislatures; and in 1832 sat the first of the great national nominating conventions.

There was, therefore, one form of congressional government which did not succeed. It was a very logical mode of party government, that of nominating the chief magistrate by congressional caucus, but it was not an open enough way. The French chamber does not select premiers by shutting up the members of its majority in caucus. Neither does the House of Commons. Their selection is made by long and open trial, in debate and in business management, of the men in whom they discover most tact for leading and most skill for planning, as well as most power for ruling. They do not say, by vote, give us M. Ferry, give us Mr. Gladstone; but Her Majesty knows as well as her subjects know that Mr. Gladstone is the only man whom the Liberal majority will obey; and President Grévy perceives that M. Ferry is the only man whom the Chambers can be made to follow. Each has elected himself by winning the first place in his party. The election has openly progressed for years, and is quite different from the private vote of a caucus about an outsider who is to sit, not in Congress, but in the executive mansion; who is not their man, but the people's.

Nor would nominations by state legislatures answer any rational purpose. Of course every State had, or thought she had,—which is much the same thing,—some citizen worthy to become President; and it would have been confusion worse confounded to have had as many candidates as there might be States. So universal a competition between "favorite sons" would have thrown the election into the House of Representatives so regularly as to replace the nominating caucus by an electing caucus.

The virtual election of the cabinet, the real executive, or at least the Prime Minister, the real head of the executive, by the Commons in England, furnishes us with a contrast rather than with a parallel to the election of our premier, the head of our executive, by a deliberative, representative body, because of the difference of function and of tenure between our Presidents and English Prime Ministers. William Pitt was elected to rule the House of Commons, John Adams to hold a constitutional balance against the Houses of Congress. The one was the leader of the legislature; the other, so to say, the colleague of the legislature. Besides, the Commons can not only make but also unmake Ministries; whilst conventions can do nothing but bind their parties by nomination, and nothing short of a well-nigh impossible impeachment can unmake a President, except four successions of the seasons. As has been very happily said by a shrewd critic, our system is essentially astronomical. A President's usefulness is measured, not by efficiency, but by calendar months. It is reckoned that if he be good at all he will be good for four years. A Prime

Minister must keep himself in favor with the majority, a President need only keep alive.

Once the functions of a presidential elector were very august. He was to speak for the people; they were to accept his judgment as theirs. He was to be as eminent in the qualities which win trust as was the greatest of the Imperial Electors in the power which inspires fear. But now he is merely a registering machine,—a sort of bell-punch to the hand of his party convention. It gives the pressure, and he rings. It is, therefore, patent to every one that that portion of the Constitution which prescribes his functions is as though it were not. A very simple and natural process of party organization, taking form first in congressional caucuses and later in nominating conventions, has radically altered a Constitution which declares that it can be amended only by the concurrence of two thirds of Congress and three fourths of the States. The sagacious men of the constitutional convention of 1787 certainly expected their work to be altered, but can hardly have expected it to be changed in so informal a manner.

The conditions which determine the choice of a nominating convention which names a President are radically different from the conditions which facilitate the choice of a representative chamber which selects for itself a Prime Minister. "Among the great purposes of a national parliament are these two," says Mr. Parton: [2] "first, to train men for practical statesmanship; and secondly, to exhibit them to the country, so that, when men of ability are wanted, they can be found without anxious search and perilous trial." In those governments which are administered by an executive committee of the legislative body, not only this training but also this exhibition is constant and complete. The career which leads to cabinet office is a career of self-exhibition. The self-revelation is made in debate, and so is made to the nation at large as well as to the Ministry of the day, who are looking out for able recruits, and to the Commons, whose ear is quick to tell a voice which it will consent to hear, a knowledge which it will pause to heed. But in governments like our own, in which legislative and executive services are altogether dissociated, this training is incomplete, and this exhibition almost entirely wanting. A nominating convention does not look over the rolls of Congress to pick a man to suit its purpose; and if it did it could not find him, because Congress is not a school for the preparation of administrators, and the convention is supposed to be searching not for an experienced committeeman, but for a tried statesman. The proper test for its application is not the test by which congressmen are assayed. They make laws, but they do not have to order the execution of the laws they make. They have a great deal of experience in directing, but none at all in being directed. Their care is to pass bills, not to keep them in running order after they have become statutes. They spend their lives without having anything to do directly with administration, though administration is dependent upon the measures which they enact.

A Presidential convention, therefore, when it nominates a man who is, or has been, a member of Congress, does not nominate him because of his congressional experience, but because it is thought that he has other abilities which were not called out in Congress. Andrew Jackson had been a member of Congress, but he was chosen President because he had won the battle of New Orleans and had driven the Indians from Florida. It was thought that his military genius evinced executive genius. The men whose fame rests altogether upon laurels won in Congress have seldom been more successful than Webster and Henry Clay in their candidacy for the chief magistracy. Washington was a soldier; Jefferson cut but a sorry figure in debate; Monroe was a diplomatist; it required diligent inquiry to find out what many of our Presidents had been before they became candidates; and eminency in legislative service has always been at best but an uncertain road to official preferment.

Of late years a tendency is observable which seems to be making the gubernatorial chairs of the greater States the nearest offices to the Presidency; and it cannot but be allowed that there is much that is rational in the tendency. The governorship of a State is very like a smaller Presidency; or, rather, the Presidency is very like a big governorship. Training in the duties of the one fits for the duties of the other. This is the only avenue of subordinate place through which the highest place can be naturally reached. Under the cabinet governments abroad a still more natural line of promotion is arranged. The Ministry is a legislative Ministry, and draws its life from the legislature, where strong talents always secure executive place. A long career in Parliament is at least a long contact with practical statesmanship, and at best a long schooling in the duties of the practical statesman. But with us there is no such intimate relationship between legislative and executive service. From experience in state administration to trial in the larger sphere of federal administration is the only natural order of promotion. We ought, therefore, to hail the recognition of this fact as in keeping with the general plan of the federal Constitution. The business of the President, occasionally great, is usually not much above routine. Most of the time it is *mere* administration, mere obedience of directions from the masters of policy, the Standing Committees. Except in so far as his power of veto constitutes him a part of the legislature, the President might, not inconveniently, be a permanent officer; the first official of a carefully-graded and impartially regulated civil service system, through whose sure series of merit-promotions the youngest clerk might rise even to the chief magistracy.[3] He is part of the official rather than of the political machinery of the government, and his duties call rather for training than for constructive genius. If there can be found in the official systems of the States a lower grade of service in which men may be advantageously drilled for Presidential functions, so much the better. The States will have better governors, the Union better Presidents, and there will have been supplied one of the most serious needs left unsupplied by the Constitution,—the need for a proper school in which to rear federal administrators.

Administration is something that men must learn, not something to skill in which they are born. Americans take to business of all kinds more naturally than any other nation ever did, and the executive duties of government constitute just an exalted kind of business; but even Americans are not Presidents in their cradles. One cannot have too much preparatory training and experience who is to fill so high a magistracy. It is difficult to perceive, therefore, upon what safe ground of reason are built the opinions of those persons who regard short terms of service as sacredly and peculiarly republican in principle. If republicanism is founded upon good sense, nothing so far removed from good sense can be part and parcel of it. Efficiency is the only just foundation for confidence in a public officer, under republican institutions no less than under monarchs; and short terms which cut off the efficient as surely and inexorably as the inefficient are quite as repugnant to republican as to monarchical rules of wisdom. Unhappily, however, this is not American doctrine. A President is dismissed almost as soon as he has learned the duties of his office, and a man who has served a dozen terms in Congress is a curiosity. We are too apt to think both the work of legislation and the work of administration easy enough to be done readily, with or without preparation, by any man of discretion and character. No one imagines that the drygoods or the hardware trade, or even the cobbler's craft, can be successfully conducted except by those who have worked through a laborious and unremunerative apprenticeship, and who have devoted their lives to perfecting themselves as tradesmen or as menders of shoes. But legislation is esteemed a thing which may be taken up with success by any shrewd man of middle age, which a lawyer may now and again advantageously combine with his practice, or of which any intelligent youth may easily catch the knack; and administration is regarded as something which an old soldier, an ex-diplomatist, or a popular politician may be trusted to take to by instinct. No man of tolerable talents need despair of having been born a Presidential candidate.

These must be pronounced very extraordinary conclusions for an eminently practical people to have accepted; and it must be received as an awakening of good sense that there is nowadays a decided inclination manifested on the part of the nation to supply training-schools for the Presidency in like minor offices, such as the governorships of the greater States. For the sort of Presidents needed under the present arrangement of our federal government, it is best to choose amongst the ablest and most experienced state governors.

So much for nomination and election. But, after election, what then? The President is not all of the Executive. He cannot get along without the men whom he appoints, with and by the consent and advice of the Senate; and they are really integral parts of that branch of the government which he titularly contains in his one single person. The characters and training of the Secretaries are of almost as much importance as his own gifts and antecedents; so that his appointment and the Senate's confirmation must be added to the machinery of nomination by convention and election by automatic electors before the whole process of making up a working executive has been noted. The early Congresses seem to have regarded the Attorney-General and the four Secretaries[4] who constituted the first Cabinets as something more than the President's lieutenants. Before the republican reaction which followed the supremacy of the Federalists, the heads of the departments appeared in person before the Houses to impart desired information, and to make what suggestions they might have to venture, just as the President attended in person to read his "address." They were always recognized units in the system, never mere ciphers to the Presidential figure which led them. Their wills counted as independent wills.

The limits of this independence would seem, however, never to have been very clearly defined. Whether or not the President was to take the advice of his appointees and colleagues appears to have depended always upon the character and temper of the President. Here, for example, is what was reported in 1862. "We pretend to no state secrets," said the New York "Evening Post," [5] "but we have been told, upon what we deem good authority, that no such thing as a combined, unitary, deliberative administration exists; that the President's brave willingness to take all responsibility has quite neutralized the idea of a joint responsibility; and that orders of the highest importance are issued, and movements commanded, which cabinet officers learn of as other people do, or, what is worse, which the cabinet officers disapprove and protest against. Each cabinet officer, again, controls his own department pretty much as he pleases, without consultation with the President or with his coadjutors, and often in the face of determinations which have been reached by the others." A picture this which forcibly reminds one of a certain imperious Prime Minister, in his last days created Earl of Chatham. These reports may have been true or they may have been mere rumors; but they depict a perfectly possible state of affairs. There is no influence except the ascendancy or tact of the President himself to keep a Cabinet in harmony and to dispose it to coöperation; so that it would be very difficult to lay down any rules as to what elements really constitute an Executive. Those elements can be determined exactly of only one administration at a time, and of that only after it has closed, and some one who knows its secrets has come forward to tell them. We think of Mr. Lincoln rather than of his Secretaries when we look back to the policy of the war-time; but we think of Mr. Hamilton rather than of President Washington when we look back to the policy of the first administration. Daniel Webster was bigger than President Fillmore, and President Jackson was bigger than Mr. Secretary Van Buren. It depends for the most part upon the character and training, the previous station, of the cabinet officers, whether or not they act as governing factors in administration, just as it depends upon the President's talents and preparatory schooling whether or not he is a mere figure-head. A weak President may prove himself wiser than the convention which nominated him, by overshadowing himself with a Cabinet of notables.

From the necessity of the case, however, the President cannot often be really supreme in matters of administration, except as the Speaker of the House of Representatives is supreme in legislation, as appointer of those who are supreme in its several departments. The President is no greater than his prerogative of veto makes him; he is, in other words, powerful rather as a branch of the legislature than as the titular head of the Executive. Almost all distinctively executive functions are specifically bestowed upon the heads of the departments. No President, however earnest and industrious, can keep the Navy in a state of creditable efficiency if he have a corrupt or incapable Secretary in the Navy Department; he cannot prevent the army from suffering the damage of demoralization if the Secretary of War is without either ability, experience, or conscience; there will be corrupt jobs in the Department of Justice, do what he will to correct the methods of a deceived or deceitful Attorney-General; he cannot secure even-handed equity for the Indian tribes if the Secretary of the Interior chooses to thwart him; and the Secretary of State may do as much mischief behind his back as can the Secretary of the Treasury. He might master the details and so control the administration of some one of the departments, but he can scarcely oversee them all with any degree of strictness. His knowledge of what they have done or are doing comes, of course, from the Secretaries themselves, and his annual messages to Congress are in large part but a recapitulation of the chief contents of the detailed reports which the heads of the departments themselves submit at the same time to the Houses.

It is easy, however, to exaggerate the power of the Cabinet. After all has been said, it is evident that they differ from the permanent officials only in not being permanent. Their tenure of office is made to depend upon the supposition that their functions are political rather than simply ministerial, independent rather than merely instrumental. They are made party representatives because of the fiction that they direct policy. In reality the First Comptroller of the Treasury has almost, if not quite, as much weight in directing departmental business as has the Secretary of the Treasury himself, and it would practically be quite as useful to have his office, which is in intention permanent, vacated by every change of administration as to have that rule with regard to the office of his official chief. The permanent organization, the clerical forces of the departments, have in the Secretaries a sort of *sliding top;* though it would probably be just as convenient in practice to have this lid permanent as to have it movable. That the Secretaries are not in fact the directors of the executive policy of the government, I have shown in pointing out the thoroughgoing supervision of even the details of administration which it is the disposition of the Standing Committees of Congress to exercise. In the actual control of affairs no one can do very much without gaining the ears of the Committees. The heads of the departments could, of course, act much more wisely in many matters than the Committees can, because they have an intimacy with the workings and the wants of those departments which no Committee can possibly possess. But Committees prefer to govern in the dark rather than not to govern at all, and the Secretaries, as a matter of fact, find themselves bound in all things larger than routine details by laws which have been made for them and which they have no legitimate means of modifying.

Of course the Secretaries are in the leading-strings of statutes, and all their duties look towards a strict obedience to Congress. Congress made them and can unmake them. It is to Congress that they must render account for the conduct of administration. The head of each department must every year make a detailed report of the expenditures of the department, and a minute account of the facilities of work and the division of functions in the department, naming each clerk of its force. The chief duties of one cabinet officer will serve to illustrate the chief duties of his colleagues. It is the duty of the Secretary of the Treasury[6] "to prepare plans for the improvement and management of the revenue and for the support of the public credit; to prescribe forms of keeping and rendering all public accounts; to grant all warrants for moneys to be issued from the Treasury in pursuance of appropriations made by Congress; to report to the Senate or House, in person or in writing, information required by them pertaining to his office; and to perform all duties relating to finance that he shall be directed to perform." "He is required to report to Congress annually, on the first Monday in June, the results of the information compiled by the Bureau of Statistics, showing the condition of manufactures, domestic trade, currency, and banks in the several States and Territories." "He prescribes regulations for the killing in Alaska Territory and adjacent waters of minks, martens, sable, and other fur-bearing animals." "And he must lay before Congress each session the reports of the Auditors, showing the applications of the appropriations made for the War and Navy Departments, and also abstracts and tabulated forms showing separate accounts of the moneys received from internal duties."

Of course it is of the utmost importance that a Secretary who has within his choice some of the minor plans for the management of the revenue and for the maintenance of the public credit should be carefully chosen from amongst men skilled in financial administration and experienced in business regulation; but it is no more necessary that the man selected for such responsible duties should be an active politician, called to preside over his department only so long as the President who appointed him continues to hold office and to like him, than it is to have a strictly political officer to fulfill his other duty of prescribing game laws for Alaska and Alaskan waters. Fur-bearing animals can have no connection with political parties,—except, perhaps, as "spoils." Indeed, it is a positive disadvantage that Mr. Secretary should be chosen upon such a principle. He cannot have the knowledge, and must therefore lack the efficiency, of a permanent official separated from the partisan conflicts of politics and advanced to the highest office of his department by a regular series of promotions won by long service. The general policy of the government in matters of finance, everything that affects the greater operations of the Treasury, depends upon legislation, and is altogether in the hands of the Committees of Ways and Means and of Finance; so that it is entirely apart from good sense to make an essentially political office out of the post of that officer who controls only administrative details.

And this remark would seem to apply with still greater force to the offices of the other Secretaries. They have even less energetic scope than the Secretary of the Treasury has. There must under any system be considerable power in the hands of the officer who handles and dispenses vast revenues, even though he handle and dispense them as directed by his employers. Money in its goings to and fro makes various mares go by the way, so to speak. It cannot move in great quantities without moving a large part of the commercial world with it. Management even of financial details may be made instrumental in turning the money-markets upside down. The Secretary of the Treasury is, therefore, less a mere chief clerk than are his coadjutors; and if his duties are not properly political, theirs certainly are not.

In view of this peculiarity of the Secretaries, in being appointed as partisans and endowed as mere officials, it is interesting to inquire what and whom they represent. They are clearly meant to represent the political party to which they belong; but it very often happens that it is impossible for them to do so. They must sometimes obey the opposite party. It is our habit to speak of the party to which the President is known to adhere and which has control of appointments to the offices of the civil service as "the party in power"; but it is very evident that control of the executive machinery is not all or even a very large part of power in a country ruled as ours is. In so far as the President is an executive officer he is the servant of Congress; and the members of the Cabinet, being confined to executive functions, are altogether the servants of Congress. The President, however, besides being titular head of the executive service, is to the extent of his veto a third branch of the legislature, and the party which he represents is in power in the same sense that it would be in power if it had on its side a majority of the members of either of the other two branches of Congress. If the House and Senate are of one party and the President and his ministers of the opposite, the President's party can hardly be said to be in power beyond the hindering and thwarting faculty of the veto. The Democrats were in power during the sessions of the Twenty-fifth Congress because they had a majority in the Senate as well as Andrew Jackson in the White House; but later Presidents have had both House and Senate against them.[7]

It is this constant possibility of party diversity between the Executive and Congress which so much complicates our system of party government. The history of administrations is not necessarily the history of parties. Presidential elections may turn the scale of party ascendency one way, and the intermediate congressional elections may quite reverse the balance. A strong party administration, by which the energy of the State is concentrated in the hands of a single well-recognized political organization, which is by reason of its power saddled with all responsibility, may sometimes be possible, but it must often be impossible. We are thus shut out in part from real party government such as we desire, and such as it is unquestionably desirable to set up in every system like ours. Party government can exist only when the absolute control of administration, the appointment of its officers as well as the direction of its means and policy, is given immediately into the hands of that branch of the government whose power is paramount, the representative body. Roger Sherman, whose perception was amongst the keenest and whose sagacity was amongst the surest in the great Convention of 1787, was very bold and outspoken in declaring this fact and in proposing to give it candid recognition. Perceiving very clearly the omnipotence which must inevitably belong to a national Congress such as the convention was about to create, he avowed that "he considered the executive magistracy as nothing more than an institution for carrying the will of the legislature into effect; that the person or persons [who should constitute the executive] ought to be appointed by, and accountable to, the legislature only, which was the depository of the supreme will of the society." Indeed, the executive was in his view so entirely the servant of the legislative will that he saw good reason to think that the legislature should judge of the number of persons of which the executive should be composed; and there seem to have been others in the convention who went along with him in substantial agreement as to these matters. It would seem to have been only a desire for the creation of as many as possible of those balances of power which now decorate the "literary theory" of the Constitution which they made that prevented a universal acquiescence in these views.

The anomaly which has resulted is seen most clearly in the party relations of the President and his Cabinet. The President is a partisan,—is elected because he is a partisan,—and yet he not infrequently negatives the legislation passed by the party whom he represents; and it may be said to be nowadays a very rare thing to find a Cabinet made up of truly representative party men. They are the men of his party whom the President likes, but not necessarily or always the men whom that party relishes. So low, indeed, has the reputation of some of our later Cabinets fallen, even in the eyes of men of their own political connection, that writers in the best of our public prints feel at full liberty to speak of their members with open contempt. "When Mr. —— was made Secretary of the Navy," laughs the New York "Nation," "no one doubted that he would treat the Department as 'spoils,' and consequently nobody has been disappointed. He is one of the statesmen who can hardly conceive of a branch of the public Administration having no spoils in it." And that this separation of the Cabinet from real party influence, and from the party leadership which would seem properly to belong to its official station, is a natural result of our constitutional scheme is made patent in the fact that the Cabinet has advanced in party insignificance as the system has grown older. The connection between the early Cabinets and the early Congresses was very like the relations between leaders and their party. Both Hamilton and Gallatin led rather than obeyed the Houses; and it was many years before the suggestions of heads of departments ceased to be sure of respectful and acquiescent consideration from the legislative Committees. But as the Committees gained facility and power the leadership of the Cabinet lost ground. Congress took command of the government so soon as ever it got command of itself, and no Secretary of to-day can claim by virtue of his office recognition as a party authority. Congress looks upon advice offered to it by anybody but its own members as gratuitous impertinence.

At the same time it is quite evident that the means which Congress has of controlling the departments and of exercising the searching oversight at which it aims are limited and defective. Its intercourse with the President is restricted to the executive messages, and its intercourse with the departments has no easier channels than private consultations between executive officials and the Committees, informal interviews of the ministers with individual members of Congress, and the written correspondence which the cabinet officers from time to time address to the presiding officers of the two Houses, at stated intervals, or in response to formal resolutions of inquiry. Congress stands almost helplessly outside of the departments. Even the special, irksome, ungracious investigations which it from time to time institutes in its spasmodic endeavors to dispel or confirm suspicions of malfeasance or of wanton corruption do not afford it more than a glimpse of the inside of a small province of federal administration. Hostile or designing officials can always hold it at arm's length by dexterous evasions and concealments. It can violently disturb, but it cannot often fathom, the waters of the sea in which the bigger fish of the civil service swim and feed. Its dragnet stirs without cleansing the bottom. Unless it have at the head of the departments capable, fearless men, altogether in its confidence and entirely in sympathy with its designs, it is clearly helpless to do more than affright those officials whose consciences are their accusers.

And it is easy to see how the commands as well as the questions of Congress may be evaded, if not directly disobeyed, by the executive agents. Its Committees may command, but they cannot superintend the execution of their commands. The Secretaries, though not free enough to have any independent policy of their own, are free enough to be very poor, because very unmanageable, servants. Once installed, their hold upon their offices does not depend upon the will of Congress. If they please the President, and keep upon living terms with their colleagues, they need not seriously regard the displeasure of the Houses, unless, indeed, by actual crime, they rashly put themselves in the way of its judicial wrath. If their folly be not too overt and extravagant, their authority may continue theirs till the earth has four times made her annual journey round the sun. They may make daily blunders in administration and repeated mistakes in business, may thwart the plans of Congress in a hundred small, vexatious ways, and yet all the while snap their fingers at its dissatisfaction or displeasure. They are denied the gratification of possessiong real power, but they have the satisfaction of being secure in a petty independence which gives them a chance to be tricky and scheming. There are ways and ways of obeying; and if Congress be not pleased, why need they care? Congress did not give them their places, and cannot easily take them away.

Still it remains true that all the big affairs of the departments are conducted in obedience to the direction of the Standing Committees. The President nominates, and with legislative approval appoints, to the more important offices of the government, and the members of the Cabinet have the privilege of advising him as to matters in most of which he has no power of final action without the concurrence of the Senate; but the gist of all policy is decided by legislative, not by executive, will. It can be no great satisfaction to any man to possess the barren privilege of suggesting the best means of managing the every-day routine business of the several bureaux so long as the larger plans which that business is meant to advance are made for him by others who are set over him. If one is commanded to go to this place or to that place, and must go, will he, nil he, it can be but small solace to him that he is left free to determine whether he will ride or walk in going the journey. The only serious questions are whether or not this so great and real control exerted by Congress can be exercised efficiently and with sufficient responsibility to those whom Congress represents, and whether good government is promoted by the arrangement.

No one, I take it for granted, is disposed to disallow the principle that the representatives of the people are the proper ultimate authority in all matters of government, and that administration is merely the clerical part of government. Legislation is the originating force. It determines what shall be done; and the President, if he cannot or will not stay legislation by the use of his extraordinary power as a branch of the legislature, is plainly bound in duty to render unquestioning obedience to Congress. And if it be his duty to obey, still more is obedience the bounden duty of his subordinates. The power of making laws is in its very nature and essence the power of directing, and that power is given to Congress. The principle is without drawback, and is inseparably of a piece with all Anglo-Saxon usage; the difficulty, if there be any, must lie in the choice of means whereby to energize the principle. The natural means would seem to be the right on the part of the representative body to have all the executive servants of its will under its close and constant supervision, and to hold them to a strict accountability: in other words, to have the privilege of dismissing them whenever their service became unsatisfactory. This is the matter-of-course privilege of every other master; and if Congress does not possess it, its mastery is hampered without being denied. The executive officials are its servants all the same; the only difference is that if they prove negligent, or incapable, or deceitful servants Congress must rest content with the best that can be got out of them until its chief administrative agent, the President, chooses to appoint better. It cannot make them docile, though it may compel them to be obedient in all greater matters. In authority of rule Congress is made master, but in means of rule it is made mere magistrate. It commands with absolute lordship, but it can discipline for disobedience only by slow and formal judicial process.

Upon Machiavelli's declaration that "nothing is more important to the stability of the state than that facility should be given by its constitution for the accusation of those who are supposed to have committed any public wrong," a writer in the "Westminster Review" makes this thoughtful comment: "The benefit of such a provision is twofold. First, the salutary fear of the probable coming of a day of account will restrain the evil practices of some bad men and self-seekers; secondly, the legal outlet of accusation gives vent to peccant humors in the body politic, which, if checked and driven inward, would work to the utter ruin of the constitution; . . . the distinction is lost between accusation and calumny." [8] And of course it was these benefits which our federal Constitution was meant to secure by means of its machinery of impeachment. No servant of the state, not even the President himself, was to be beyond the reach of accusation by the House of Representatives and of trial by the Senate. But the processes of impeachment, like those of amendment, are ponderous and difficult to handle. It requires something like passion to set them a-going; and nothing short of the grossest offenses against the plain law of the land will suffice to give them speed and effectiveness. Indignation so great as to overcrow party interest may secure a conviction; nothing less can. Indeed, judging by our past experiences, impeachment may be said to be little more than an empty menace. The House of Representatives is a tardy grand jury, and the Senate an uncertain court.

Besides, great crimes such as might speed even impeachment are not ordinary things in the loosest public service. An open-eyed public opinion can generally give them effective check. That which usually and every day clogs and hampers good government is folly or incapacity on the part of the ministers of state. Even more necessary, therefore, than a power clothed with authority to accuse, try, and punish for public crime is some ultimate authority, whose privilege it shall be to dismiss for inefficiency. Impeachment is aimed altogether above the head of business management. A merchant would not think it fair, even if it were lawful, to shoot a clerk who could not learn the business. Dismissal is quite as effective for his purposes, and more merciful to the clerk. The crying inconvenience of our system is, therefore, that the constitutional authority whose prerogative it is to direct policy and oversee administration has fewer facilities for getting its work well done than has the humblest citizen for obtaining satisfactory aid in his own undertakings. The authority most interested in appointments and dismissals in the civil service has little to do with the one and less to do with the other. The President appoints with the sanction of the Senate, and cannot dismiss his advisers without legislative consent;[9] yet the ministers in reality serve, not the President, but Congress, and Congress can neither appoint nor dismiss. In other words, the President must in both acts take the initiative, though he is not the real master; and Congress, which is the real master, has in these vital matters only a consultative voice, which it may utter, through its upper chamber, only when its opinion is asked. I should regard my business as a hopeless undertaking if my chief agent had to be appointed by a third party, and, besides being himself put beyond my power of control, were charged with the choice and discipline of all his subordinates, subject not to my directions, but simply to my acquiescence!

The relations existing between Congress and the departments must be fatally demoralizing to both. There is and can be between them nothing like confidential and thorough coöperation. The departments may be excused for that attitude of hostility which they sometimes assume towards Congress, because it is quite human for the servant to fear and deceive the master whom he does not regard as his friend, but suspects of being a distrustful spy of his movements. Congress cannot control the officers of the executive without disgracing them. Its only whip is investigation, semi-judicial examination into corners suspected to be dirty. It must draw the public eye by openly avowing a suspicion of malfeasance, and must then magnify and intensify the scandal by setting its Committees to cross-examining scared subordinates and sulky ministers. And after all is over and the murder out, probably nothing is done. The offenders, if any one has offended, often remain in office, shamed before the world, and ruined in the estimation of all honest people, but still drawing their salaries and comfortably waiting for the short memory of the public mind to forget them. Why unearth the carcass if you cannot remove it?

Then, too, the departments frequently complain of the incessant exactions made upon them by Congress. They grumble that they are kept busy in satisfying its curiosity and in meeting the demands of its uneasy activity. The clerks have ordinarily as much as they can do in keeping afoot the usual routine business of their departments; but Congress is continually calling upon them for information which must be laboriously collected from all sorts of sources, remote and accessible. A great speech in the Senate may cost them hours of anxious toil: for the Senator who makes it is quite likely beforehand to introduce a resolution calling upon one of the Secretaries for full statistics with reference to this, that, or the other topic upon which he desires to speak. If it be finance, he must have comparative tables of taxation; if it be commerce or the tariff, he cannot dispense with any of the minutest figures of the Treasury accounts; whatever be his theme, he cannot lay his foundations more surely than upon official information, and the Senate is usually unhesitatingly ready with an easy assent to the resolution which puts the whole clerical force of the administration at his service. And of course the House too asks innumerable questions, which patient clerks and protesting Secretaries must answer to the last and most minute particular. This is what the departmental officials testily call the tyranny of Congress, and no impartial third person can reasonably forbid them the use of the word.

I know of few things harder to state clearly and within reasonable compass than just how the nation keeps control of policy in spite of these hide-and-seek vagaries of authority. Indeed, it is doubtful if it does keep control through all the roundabout paths which legislative and executive responsibility are permitted to take. It must follow Congress somewhat blindly; Congress is known to obey without altogether under-

standing its Committees: and the Committees must consign
the execution of their plans to officials who have opportunities
not a few to hoodwink them. At the end of these blind processes is it probable that the ultimate authority, the people, is
quite clear in its mind as to what has been done or what may
be done another time? Take, for example, financial policy,—
a very fair example, because, as I have shown, the legislative
stages of financial policy are more talked about than any other
congressional business, though for that reason an extreme example. If, after appropriations and adjustments of taxation
have been tardily and in much tribulation of scheming and
argument agreed upon by the House, the imperative suggestions and stubborn insistence of the Senate confuse matters till
hardly the Conference Committees themselves know clearly
what the outcome of the disagreements has been; and if, when
these compromise measures are launched as laws, the method
of their execution is beyond the view of the Houses, in the
semi-privacy of the departments, how is the comprehension—
not to speak of the will—of the people to keep any sort of
hold upon the course of affairs? There are no screws of responsibility which they can turn upon the consciences or upon
the official thumbs of the congressional Committees principally
concerned. Congressional Committees are nothing to the nation; they are only pieces of the interior mechanism of Congress. To Congress they stand or fall. And, since Congress
itself can scarcely be sure of having its own way with them,
the constituencies are manifestly unlikely to be able to govern
them. As for the departments, the people can hardly do more
in drilling them to unquestioning obedience and docile efficiency than Congress can. Congress is, and must be, in these
matters the nation's eyes and voice. If it cannot see what goes
wrong and cannot get itself heeded when it commands, the
nation likewise is both blind and dumb.

This, plainly put, is the practical result of the piecing of
authority, the cutting of it up into small bits, which is con-
trived in our constitutional system. Each branch of the government is fitted out with a small section of responsibility,
whose limited opportunities afford to the conscience of each
many easy escapes. Every suspected culprit may shift the

responsibility upon his fellows. Is Congress rated for corrupt or imperfect or foolish legislation? It may urge that it has to follow hastily its Committees or do nothing at all but talk; how can it help it if a stupid Committee leads it unawares into unjust or fatuous enterprises? Does administration blunder and run itself into all sorts of straits? The Secretaries hasten to plead the unreasonable or unwise commands of Congress, and Congress falls to blaming the Secretaries. The Secretaries aver that the whole mischief might have been avoided if they had only been allowed to suggest the proper measures; and the men who framed the existing measures in their turn avow their despair of good government so long as they must intrust all their plans to the bungling incompetence of men who are appointed by and responsible to somebody else. How is the schoolmaster, the nation, to know which boy needs the whipping?

Moreover, it is impossible to deny that this division of authority and concealment of responsibility are calculated to subject the government to a very distressing paralysis in moments of emergency. There are few, if any, important steps that can be taken by any one branch of the government without the consent or coöperation of some other branch. Congress must act through the President and his Cabinet; the President and his Cabinet must wait upon the will of Congress. There is no one supreme, ultimate head—whether magistrate or representative body—which can decide at once and with conclusive authority what shall be done at those times when some decision there must be, and that immediately. Of course this lack is of a sort to be felt at all times, in seasons of tranquil rounds of business as well as at moments of sharp crisis; but in times of sudden exigency it might prove fatal,—fatal either in breaking down the system or in failing to meet the emergency.[10] Policy cannot be either prompt or straightforward when it must serve many masters. It must either equivocate, or hesitate, or fail altogether. It may set out with clear purpose from Congress, but get waylaid or maimed by the Executive.

If there be one principle clearer than another, it is this: that in any business, whether of government or of mere merchandising, *somebody must be trusted,* in order that when things go wrong it may be quite plain who should be punished. In order to drive trade at the speed and with the success you desire, you must confide without suspicion in your chief clerk, giving him the power to ruin you, because you thereby furnish him with a motive for serving you. His reputation, his own honor or disgrace, all his own commercial prospects, hang upon your success. And human nature is much the same in government as in the dry-goods trade. *Power and strict accountability for its use* are the essential constituents of good government. A sense of highest responsibility, a dignifying and elevating sense of being trusted, together with a consciousness of being in an official station so conspicuous that no faithful discharge of duty can go unacknowledged and unrewarded, and no breach of trust undiscovered and unpunished,—these are the influences, the only influences, which foster practical, energetic, and trustworthy statesmanship. The best rulers are always those to whom great power is intrusted in such a manner as to make them feel that they will surely be abundantly honored and recompensed for a just and patriotic use of it, and to make them know that nothing can shield them from full retribution for every abuse of it.

It is, therefore, manifestly a radical defect in our federal system that it parcels out power and confuses responsibility as it does. The main purpose of the Convention of 1787 seems to have been to accomplish this grievous mistake. The "literary theory" of checks and balances is simply a consistent account of what our constitution-makers tried to do; and those checks and balances have proved mischievous just to the extent to which they have succeeded in establishing themselves as realities. It is quite safe to say that were it possible to call together again the members of that wonderful Convention to view the work of their hands in the light of the century that has tested it, they would be the first to admit that the only fruit of dividing power had been to make it irresponsible. It is just this that has made civil service reform tarry in this country and that makes it still almost doubtful of issue. We are in just the case that England was in before she achieved the reform for which we are striving. The date of the reform in England is no less significant than the fact. It was not accomplished until a distinct responsibility of the Ministers of the Crown to one, and to only one, master had been established beyond all uncertainty. This is the most striking and suggestive lesson to be gathered from Mr. Eaton's interesting and valuable history of Civil Service in Great Britain. The Reform was originated in 1853 by the Cabinet of Lord Aberdeen. It sprang from the suggestion of the appointing officers, and was carried through in the face of opposition from the House of Commons, because, paradoxically enough, the Ministry had at last come to feel their responsibility to the Commons, or rather to the nation whom the Commons represented.

Those great improvements which have been made in the public service of the British empire since the days of Walpole and Newcastle have gone hand in hand with the perfecting of the system now known as responsible Cabinet government. That system was slow in coming to perfection. It was not till long after Walpole's day that unity of responsibility on the part of the Cabinet—and that singleness of responsibility which made them look only to the Commons for authority—came to be recognized as an established constitutional principle. "As a consequence of the earlier practice of constructing Cabinets of men of different political views, it followed that the members of such Cabinets did not and could not regard their responsibility to Parliament as one and indivisible. The resignation of an important member, or even of the Prime Minister, was not regarded as necessitating the simultaneous retirement of his colleagues. Even so late as the fall of Sir Robert Walpole, fifty years after the Revolution Settlement (and itself the first instance of resignation in deference to a hostile parliamentary vote) we find the King requesting Walpole's successor, Pulteney, 'not to distress the Government by making too many changes in the midst of a session'; and Pulteney replying that he would be satisfied, provided 'the main forts of the Government,' or, in other words, the principal offices of state, were placed in his hands. It was not till the displacement of Lord North's ministry by that of Lord Rockingham in 1782 that a whole administration, with the exception of the Lord Chancellor, was changed by a vote of want of confidence passed in the House of Commons. Thenceforth, however, the resignation of the head of a Government in deference to an adverse vote of the popular chamber has invariably been accompanied by the resignation of all his colleagues." [11] But, even after the establishment of that precedent, it was still many years before Cabinets were free to please none but the Commons,—free to follow their own policies without authoritative suggestion from the sovereign. Until the death of the fourth George they were made to feel that they owed a double allegiance: to the Commons and to the King. The composition of Ministries still depended largely on the royal whim, and their actions were hampered by the necessity of steering a careful middle course between the displeasure of parliament and the ill-will of His Majesty. The present century had run far on towards the reign of Victoria before they were free to pay undivided obedience to the representatives of the people. When once they had become responsible to the Commons alone, however, and almost as soon as they were assured of their new position as the servants of the nation, they were prompted to even hazardous efforts for the reform of the civil service. They were conscious that the entire weight and responsibility of government rested upon their shoulders, and, as men regardful of the interests of the party which they represented, jealous for the preservation of their own fair names, and anxious, consequently, for the promotion of wise rule, they were naturally and of course the first to advocate a better system of appointment to that service whose chiefs they were recognized to be. They were prompt to declare that it was the "duty of the executive to provide for the efficient and harmonious working of the civil service," and that they could not "transfer that duty to any other body far less competent than themselves without infringing a great and important constitutional principle, already too often infringed, to the great detriment of the public service." They therefore determined themselves to inaugurate the merit-system without waiting for the assent of parliament, by simply surrendering their power of appointment in the various departments to a non-partisan examining board, trusting to the power of public opinion to induce parliament, after the thing had been done, to vote sufficient money to put the scheme into successful operation. And they did not reckon without their host. Reluctant as the members of the House of Commons were to resign that control of the national patronage which they had from time immemorial been accustomed to exercise by means of various crooked indirections, and which it had been their pleasure and their power to possess, they had not the face to avow their suspicious unwillingness in answer to the honorable call of a trusted Ministry who were supported in their demand by all that was honest in public sentiment, and the world was afforded the gratifying but unwonted spectacle of party leaders sacrificing to the cause of good government, freely and altogether of their own accord, the "spoils" of office so long dear to the party and to the assembly which they represented and served.

In this country the course of the reform was quite the reverse. Neither the Executive nor Congress began it. The call for it came imperatively from the people; it was a formulated demand of public opinion made upon Congress, and it had to be made again and again, each time with more determined emphasis, before Congress heeded. It worked its way up from the convictions of the many to the purposes of the few. Amongst the chief difficulties that have stood in its way, and which still block its perfect realization, is that peculiarity of structure which I have just now pointed out as intrinsic in the scheme of divided power which runs through the Constitution. One of the conditions precedent to any real and lasting reform of the civil service, in a country whose public service is moulded by the conditions of self-government, is the drawing of a sharp line of distinction between those offices which are political and those which are *non*-political. The strictest rules of business discipline, of merit-tenure and earned promotion, must rule every office whose incumbent has naught to do with choosing between policies; but no rules except the choice of parties can or should make and unmake, reward or punish, those officers whose privilege it is to fix upon the political purposes which administration shall be made to serve. These latter are not many under any form of government. There are said to be but fifty such at most in the civil service of Great Britain;

but these fifty go in or out as the balance of power shifts from party to party. In the case of our own civil service it would, I take it, be extremely hard to determine where the line should be drawn. In all the higher grades this particular distinction is quite obscured. A doubt exists as to the Cabinet itself. Are the Secretaries political or non-political officers? It would seem that they are exclusively neither. They are at least semi-political. They are, on the one hand, merely the servants of Congress, and yet, on the other hand, they have enough freedom of discretion to mar and color, if not to choose, political ends. They can wreck plans, if they cannot make them. Should they be made permanent officials because they are mere Secretaries, or should their tenure depend upon the fortunes of parties because they have many chances to render party services? And if the one rule or the other is to be applied to them, to how many, and to which of their chief subordinates, is it to be extended? If they are not properly or necessarily party men, let them pass the examinations and run the gauntlet of the usual tests of efficiency, let errand-boys work up to Secretaryships; but if not, let their responsibility to their party be made strict and determinate. That is the cardinal point of practical civil service reform.

This doubt as to the exact *status* in the system of the chief ministers of state is a most striking commentary on the system itself. Its complete self is logical and simple. But its complete self exists only in theory. Its real self offers a surprise and presents a mystery at every change of view. The practical observer who seeks for facts and actual conditions of organization is often sorely puzzled to come at the real methods of government. Pitfalls await him on every side. If constitutional lawyers of strait-laced consciences filled Congress and officered the departments, every clause of the Constitution would be accorded a formal obedience, and it would be as easy to know beforehand just what the government will be like inside tomorrow as it is now to know what it was like outside yesterday. But neither the knowledge nor the consciences of politicians keep them very close to the Constitution; and it is with politicians that we have to deal nowadays in studying the government. Every government is largely what the men are who constitute it. If the character or opinions of legislators and administrators change from time to time, the nature of the government changes with them; and as both their characters and their opinions do change very often it is very hard to make a picture of the government which can be said to have been perfectly faithful yesterday, and can be confidently expected to be exactly accurate to-morrow. Add to these embarrassments, which may be called the embarrassments of human nature, other embarrassments such as our system affords, the embarrassments of subtle legal distinctions, a fine theoretical plan made in delicate hair-lines, requirements of law which can hardly be met and can easily and naturally be evaded or disregarded, and you have in full the conception of the difficulties which attend a practical exposition of the real facts of federal administration. It is not impossible to point out what the Executive was intended to be, what it has sometimes been, or what it might be; nor is it forbidden the diligent to discover the main conditions which mould it to the forms of congressional supremacy; but more than this is not to be expected.

SIX

Political philosophy must analyze political history; it must distinguish what is due to the excellence of the people, and what to the excellence of the laws; it must carefully calculate the exact effect of each part of the constitution, though thus it may destroy many an idol of the multitude, and detect the secret of utility where but few imagined it to lie.—BAGEHOT.

CONCLUSION

Congress always makes what haste it can to legislate. It is the prime object of its rules to expedite law-making. Its customs are fruits of its characteristic diligence in enactment. Be the matters small or great, frivolous or grave, which busy it, its aim is to have laws always a-making. Its temper is strenuously legislative. That it cannot regulate all the questions to which its attention is weekly invited is its misfortune, not its fault; is due to the human limitation of its faculties, not to any narrow circumscription of its desires. If its committee machinery is inadequate to the task of bringing to action more than one out of every hundred of the bills introduced, it is not because the quick clearance of the docket is not the motive of its organic life. If legislation, therefore, were the only or the chief object for which it should live, it would not be possible to withhold admiration from those clever hurrying rules and those inexorable customs which seek to facilitate it. Nothing but a doubt as to whether or not Congress should confine itself to law-making can challenge with a question the utility of its organization as a facile statute-devising machine.

The political philosopher of these days of self-government has, however, something more than a doubt with which to gainsay the usefulness of a sovereign representative body which confines itself to legislation to the exclusion of all other functions. Buckle declared, indeed, that the chief use and value of legislation nowadays lay in its opportunity and power to remedy the mistakes of the legislation of the past; that it was beneficent only when it carried healing in its wings; that repeal was more blessed than enactment. And it is certainly true that the greater part of the labor of legislation consists in carrying the loads recklessly or bravely shouldered in times gone by, when the animal which is now a bull was only a calf, and in completing, if they may be completed, the tasks once undertaken in the shape of unambitious schemes which at the outset looked innocent enough. Having got his foot into it, the legislator finds it difficult, if not impossible, to get it out again. "The modern industrial organization, including banks, corporations, joint-stock companies, financial devices, national debts, paper currency, national systems of taxation, is largely the creation of legislation (not in its historical origin, but in the mode of its existence and in its authority), and is largely regulated by legislation. Capital is the breath of life to this organization, and every day, as the organization becomes more complex and delicate, the folly of assailing capital or credit becomes greater. At the same time it is evident that the task of the legislator to embrace in his view the whole system, to adjust his rules so that the play of the civil institutions shall not alter the play of the economic forces, requires more training and more acumen. Furthermore, the greater the complication and delicacy of the industrial system, the greater the chances for cupidity when backed by craft, and the task of the legislator to meet and defeat the attempts of this cupidity is one of constantly increasing difficulty." [1]

Legislation unquestionably generates legislation. Every statute may be said to have a long lineage of statutes behind it; and whether that lineage be honorable or of ill repute is as much a question as to each individual statute as it can be with regard to the ancestry of each individual legislator. Every statute in its turn has a numerous progeny, and only time and opportunity can decide whether its offspring will bring it honor or shame. Once begin the dance of legislation, and you must struggle through its mazes as best you can to its breathless end,—if any end there be.

It is not surprising, therefore, that the enacting, revising, tinkering, repealing of laws should engross the attention and engage the entire energy of such a body as Congress. It is, however, easy to see how it might be better employed; or, at least, how it might add others to this overshadowing function, to the infinite advantage of the government. Quite as important as legislation is vigilant oversight of administration; and even more important than legislation is the instruction and guidance in political affairs which the people might receive from a body which kept all national concerns suffused in a broad daylight of discussion. There is no similar legislature in existence which is so shut up to the one business of law-making as is our Congress. As I have said, it in a way superintends administration by the exercise of semi-judicial powers of investigation, whose limitations and insufficiency are manifest. But other national legislatures command administration and verify their name of "parliaments" by talking official acts into notoriety. Our extra-constitutional party conventions, short-lived and poor in power as they are, constitute our only machinery for that sort of control of the executive which consists in the award of personal rewards and punishments. This is the cardinal fact which differentiates Congress from the Chamber of Deputies and from Parliament, and which puts it beyond the reach of those eminently useful functions whose exercise would so raise it in usefulness and in dignity.

An effective representative body, gifted with the power to rule, ought, it would seem, not only to speak the will of the nation, which Congress does, but also to lead it to its conclusions, to utter the voice of its opinions, and to serve as its eyes in superintending all matters of government,—which Congress does not do. The discussions which take place in Congress are aimed at random. They now and again strike rather sharply the tender spots in this, that, or the other measure; but, as I have said, no two measures consciously join in purpose or agree in character, and so debate must wander as widely as the subjects of debate. Since there is little coherency about the legislation agreed upon, there can be little coherency about the debates. There is no one policy to be attacked or defended, but only a score or two of separate bills. To attend to such discussions is uninteresting; to be instructed by them is impossible. There is some scandal and discomfort, but infinite advantage, in having every affair of administration subjected to the test of constant examination on the part of the assembly which represents the nation. The chief use of such inquisition is, not the direction of those affairs in a way with which the country will be satisfied (though that itself is of course all-important), but the enlightenment of the people, which is always its sure consequence. Very few men are unequal to a danger which they see and understand; all men quail before a threatening which is dark and unintelligible, and suspect what is done behind a screen. If the people could have, through Congress, daily knowledge of all the more important transactions of the governmental offices, an insight into all that now seems withheld and private, their confidence in the executive, now so often shaken, would, I think, be very soon established. Because dishonesty *can* lurk under the privacies now vouchsafed our administrative agents, much that is upright and pure suffers unjust suspicion. Discoveries of guilt in a bureau cloud with doubts the trustworthiness of a department. As nothing is open enough for the quick and easy detection of peculation or fraud, so nothing is open enough for the due vindication and acknowledgment of honesty. The isolation and privacy which shield the one from discovery cheat the other of reward.

Inquisitiveness is never so forward, enterprising, and irrepressible as in a popular assembly which is given leave to ask questions and is afforded ready and abundant means of getting its questions answered. No cross-examination is more searching than that to which a minister of the Crown is subjected by the all-curious Commons. "Sir Robert Peel once asked to have a number of questions carefully written down which they asked him one day in succession in the House of Commons. They seemed a list of everything that could occur in the British empire or to the brain of a member of parliament." [2] If one considered only the wear and tear upon ministers of state, which the plague of constant interrogation must inflict, he could wish that their lives, if useful, might be spared this blight of unending explanation; but no one can overestimate the immense advantage of a facility so unlimited for knowing all that is going on in the places where authority lives. The conscience of every member of the representative body is at the service of the nation. All that he feels bound to know he can find out; and what he finds out goes to the ears of the country. The question is his, the answer the nation's. And the inquisitiveness of such bodies as Congress is the best conceivable source of information. Congress is the only body which has the proper motive for inquiry, and it is the only body which has the power to act effectively upon the knowledge which its inquiries secure. The Press is merely curious or merely partisan. The people are scattered and unorganized. But Congress is, as it were, the corporate people, the mouthpiece of its will. It is a sovereign delegation which could ask questions with dignity, because with authority and with power to act.

Congress is fast becoming the governing body of the nation, and yet the only power which it possesses in perfection is the power which is but a part of government, the power of legislation. Legislation is but the oil of government. It is that which lubricates its channels and speeds its wheels; that which lessens the friction and so eases the movement. Or perhaps I shall be admitted to have hit upon a closer and apter analogy if I say that legislation is like a foreman set over the forces of government. It issues the orders which others obey. It directs, it admonishes, but it does not do the actual heavy work of governing. A good foreman does, it is true, himself take a hand in the work which he guides; and so I suppose our legislation must be likened to a poor foreman, because it stands altogether apart from that work which it is set to see well done. Members of Congress ought not to be censured too severely, however, when they fail to check evil courses on the part of the executive. They have been denied the means of doing so promptly and with effect. Whatever intention may have controlled the compromises of constitution-making in 1787, their result was to give us, not government by discussion, which is the only tolerable sort of government for a people which tries to do its own governing, but only *legislation* by discussion, which is no more than a small part of government by discussion. What is quite as indispensable as the debate of problems of legislation is the debate of all matters of administration. It is even more important to know how the house is being built than to know how the plans of the architect were conceived and how his specifications were calculated. It is better to have skillful work—stout walls, reliable arches, unbending rafters, and windows sure to "expel the winter's flaw"—than a drawing on paper which is the admiration of all the practical artists in the country. The discipline of an army depends quite as much upon the temper of the troops as upon the orders of the day.

It is the proper duty of a representative body to look diligently into every affair of government and to talk much about what it sees. It is meant to be the eyes and the voice, and to embody the wisdom and will of its constituents. Unless Congress have and use every means of acquainting itself with the acts and the disposition of the administrative agents of the government, the country must be helpless to learn how it is being served; and unless Congress both scrutinize these things and sift them by every form of discussion, the country must remain in embarrassing, crippling ignorance of the very affairs which it is most important that it should understand and direct. The informing function of Congress should be preferred even to its legislative function. The argument is not only that discussed and interrogated administration is the only pure and efficient administration, but, more than that, that the only really self-governing people is that people which discusses and interrogates its administration. The talk on the part of Congress which we sometimes justly condemn is the profitless squabble of words over frivolous bills or selfish party issues. It would be hard to conceive of there being too much talk about the practical concerns and processes of government. Such talk it is which, when earnestly and purposefully conducted, clears the public mind and shapes the demands of public opinion.

Congress could not be too diligent about such talking; whereas it may easily be too diligent in legislation. It often overdoes that business. It already sends to its Committees bills too many by the thousand to be given even a hasty thought; but its immense committee facilities and the absence of all other duties but that of legislation make it omnivorous in its appetite for new subjects for consideration. It is greedy to have a taste of every possible dish that may be put upon its table, as an "extra" to the constitutional bill of fare. This disposition on its part is the more notable because there is certainly less need for it to hurry and overwork itself at lawmaking than exists in the case of most other great national legislatures. It is not state and national legislature combined, as are the Commons of England and the Chambers of France. Like the Reichstag of our cousin Germans, it is restricted to subjects of imperial scope. Its thoughts are meant to be kept for national interests. Its time is spared the waste of attention to local affairs. It is even forbidden the vast domain of the laws of property, of commercial dealing, and of ordinary crime. And even in the matter of caring for national interests the way has from the first been made plain and easy for it. There are no clogging feudal institutions to embarrass it. There is no long-continued practice of legal or of royal tyranny for it to cure,—no clearing away of old débris of any sort to delay it in its exercise of a common-sense dominion over a thoroughly modern and progressive nation. It is easy to believe that its legislative purposes might be most fortunately clarified and simplified, were it to square them by a conscientious attention to the paramount and controlling duty of understanding, discussing, and directing administration.

If the people's authorized representatives do not take upon themselves this duty, and by identifying themselves with the actual work of government stand between it and irresponsible, half-informed criticism, to what harassments is the executive not exposed? Led and checked by Congress, the prurient and fearless, because anonymous, animadversions of the Press, now so often premature and inconsiderate, might be disciplined into serviceable capacity to interpret and judge. Its energy and sagacity might be tempered by discretion, and strengthened by knowledge. One of our chief constitutional difficulties is that, in opportunities for informing and guiding public opinion, the freedom of the Press is greater than the freedom of Congress. It is as if newspapers, instead of the board of directors, were the sources of information for the stockholders of a corporation. We look into correspondents' letters instead of into the Congressional Record to find out what is a-doing and a-planning in the departments. Congress is altogether excluded from the arrangement by which the Press declares what the executive is, and conventions of the national parties decide what the executive shall be. Editors are self-constituted our guides, and caucus delegates our government directors.

Since all this curious scattering of functions and contrivance of frail, extra-constitutional machinery of government is the result of that entire separation of the legislative and executive branches of the system which is with us so characteristically and essentially constitutional, it is exceedingly interesting to inquire and important to understand how that separation came to be insisted upon in the making of the Constitution. Alexander Hamilton has in our own times, as well as before, been "severely reproached with having said that the British government was the 'best model in existence.' In 1787 this was a mere truism. However much the men of that day differed they were all agreed in despising and distrusting *a priori* constitutions and ideally perfect governments, fresh from the brains of visionary enthusiasts, such as sprang up rankly in the soil of the French revolution. The Convention of 1787 was composed of very able men of the English-speaking race. They took the system of government with which they had been familiar, improved it, adapted it to the circumstances with which they had to deal, and put it into successful operation. Hamilton's plan, then, like the others, was on the British model, and it did not differ essentially in details from that finally adopted." [3] It is needful, however, to remember in this connection what has already been alluded to, that when that convention was copying the English Constitution, that Constitution was in a stage of transition, and had by no means fully developed the features which are now recognized as most characteristic of it. Mr. Lodge is quite right in saying that the

Convention, in adapting, improved upon the English Constitution with which its members were familiar,—the Constitution of George III. and Lord North, the Constitution which had failed to crush Bute. It could hardly be said with equal confidence, however, that our system as then made was an improvement upon that scheme of responsible cabinet government which challenges the admiration of the world to-day, though it was quite plainly a marked advance upon a parliament of royal nominees and pensionaries and a secret cabinet of "king's friends." The English Constitution of that day had a great many features which did not invite republican imitation. It was suspected, if not known, that the ministers who sat in parliament were little more than the tools of a ministry of royal favorites who were kept out of sight behind the strictest confidences of the court. It was notorious that the subservient parliaments of the day represented the estates and the money of the peers and the influence of the King rather than the intelligence and purpose of the nation. The whole "form and pressure" of the time illustrated only too forcibly Lord Bute's sinister suggestion, that "the forms of a free and the ends of an arbitrary government are things not altogether incompatible." It was, therefore, perfectly natural that the warnings to be so easily drawn from the sight of a despotic monarch binding the usages and privileges of self-government to the service of his own intemperate purposes should be given grave heed by Americans, who were the very persons who had suffered most from the existing abuses. It was something more than natural that the Convention of 1787 should desire to erect a Congress which would not be subservient and an executive which could not be despotic. And it was equally to have been expected that they should regard an absolute separation of these two great branches of the system as the only effectual means for the accomplishment of that much desired end. It was impossible that they could believe that executive and legislature could be brought into close relations of coöperation and mutual confidence without being tempted, nay, even bidden, to collude. How could either maintain its independence of action unless each were to have the guaranty of the Constitution that its own domain should be absolutely safe from invasion, its own prerogatives absolutely free from challenge? "They shrank from placing sovereign power anywhere. They feared that it would generate tyranny; George III. had been a tyrant to them, and come what might they would not make a George III." [4] They would conquer, by dividing, the power they so much feared to see in any single hand.

"The English Constitution, in a word," says our most astute English critic, "is framed on the principle of choosing a single sovereign authority, and making it good; the American, upon the principle of having many sovereign authorities, and hoping that their multitude may atone for their inferiority. The Americans now extol their institutions, and so defraud themselves of their due praise. But if they had not a genius for politics, if they had not a moderation in action singularly curious where superficial speech is so violent, if they had not a regard for law, such as no great people have ever evinced, and infinitely surpassing ours, the multiplicity of authorities in the American Constitution would long ago have brought it to a bad end. Sensible shareholders, I have heard a shrewd attorney say, can work *any* deed of settlement; and so the men of Massachusetts could, I believe, work *any* constitution." [5] It is not necessary to assent to Mr. Bagehot's strictures; but it is not possible to deny the clear-sighted justice of this criticism. In order to be fair to the memory of our great constitution-makers, however, it is necessary to remember that when they sat in convention in Philadelphia the English Constitution, which they copied, was not the simple system which was before Mr. Bagehot's eyes when he wrote. Its single sovereign authority was not then a twice-reformed House of Commons truly representative of the nation and readily obeyed by a responsible Ministry. The sovereignty was at see-saw between the throne and the parliament,—and the throne-end of the beam was generally uppermost. Our device of separated, individualized powers was very much better than a nominal sovereignty of the Commons which was suffered to be overridden by force, fraud, or craft, by the real sovereignty of the King. The English Constitution was at that time in reality much worse than our own; and, if it is now superior, it is so because its growth has not been hindered or destroyed by the too tight ligaments of a written fundamental law.

The natural, the inevitable tendency of every system of self-government like our own and the British is to exalt the representative body, the people's parliament, to a position of absolute supremacy. That tendency has, I think, been quite as marked in our own constitutional history as in that of any other country, though its power has been to some extent neutralized, and its progress in great part stayed, by those denials of that supremacy which we respect because they are written in our law. The political law written in our hearts is here at variance with that which the Constitution sought to establish. A written constitution may and often will be violated in both letter and spirit by a people of energetic political talents and a keen instinct for progressive practical development; but so long as they adhere to the forms of such a constitution, so long as the machinery of government supplied by it is the only machinery which the legal and moral sense of such a people permits it to use, its political development must be in many directions narrowly restricted because of an insuperable lack of open or adequate channels. Our Constitution, like every other constitution which puts the authority to make laws and the duty of controlling the public expenditure into the hands of a popular assembly, practically sets that assembly to rule the affairs of the nation as supreme overlord. But, by separating it entirely from its executive agencies, it deprives it of the opportunity and means for making its authority complete and convenient. The constitutional machinery is left of such a pattern that other forces less than that of Congress may cross and compete with Congress, though they are too small to overcome or long offset it; and the result is simply an unpleasant, wearing friction which, with other adjustments, more felicitous and equally safe, might readily be avoided.

Congress, consequently, is still lingering and chafing under just such embarrassments as made the English Commons a nuisance both to themselves and to everybody else immediately after the Revolution Settlement had given them their first sure promise of supremacy. The parallel is startlingly exact. "In outer seeming the Revolution of 1688 had only transferred the sovereignty over England from James to William and Mary. In actual fact it had given a powerful and decisive impulse to the great constitutional progress which was transferring the sovereignty from the King to the House of Commons. From the moment when its sole right to tax the nation was established by the Bill of Rights, and when its own resolve settled the practice of granting none but annual supplies to the Crown, the House of Commons became the supreme power in the State. . . . But though the constitutional change was complete, the machinery of government was far from having adapted itself to the new conditions of political life which such a change brought about. However powerful the will of the Commons might be, it had no means of bringing its will directly to bear on the control of public affairs. The ministers who had charge of them were not its servants but the servants of the Crown; it was from the King that they looked for direction, and to the King that they held themselves responsible. By impeachment or more indirect means the Commons could force a king to remove a minister who contradicted their will; but they had no constitutional power to replace the fallen statesman by a minister who would carry out their will.

"The result was the growth of a temper in the Lower House which drove William and his ministers to despair. It became as corrupt, as jealous of power, as fickle in its resolves and factious in its spirit as bodies always become whose consciousness of the possession of power is untempered by a corresponding consciousness of the practical difficulties or the moral responsibilities of the power which they possess. It grumbled . . . and it blamed the Crown and its ministers for all at which it grumbled. But it was hard to find out what policy or measures it would have preferred. Its mood changed, as William bitterly complained, with every hour. . . . The Houses were in fact without the guidance of recognized leaders, without adequate information, and destitute of that organization out of which alone a definite policy can come." [6]

The cure for this state of things which Sunderland had the sagacity to suggest, and William the wisdom to apply, was the mediation between King and Commons of a cabinet representative of the majority of the popular chamber,—a first but long and decisive step towards responsible cabinet government. Whether a similar remedy would be possible or desirable in our own case it is altogether aside from my present purpose to inquire. I am pointing out facts,—diagnosing, not prescribing remedies. My only point just now is, that no one can help being struck by the closeness of the likeness between the incipient distempers of the first parliaments of William and Mary and the developed disorders now so plainly discernible in the constitution of Congress. Though honest and diligent, it is meddlesome and inefficient; and it is meddlesome and inefficient for exactly the same reasons that made it natural that the post-Revolutionary parliaments should exhibit like clumsiness and like temper: namely, because it is "without the guidance of recognized leaders, without adequate information, and destitute of that organization out of which alone a definite policy can come."

The dangers of this serious imperfection in our governmental machinery have not been clearly demonstrated in our experience hitherto; but now their delayed fulfillment seems to be close at hand. The plain tendency is towards a centralization of all the greater powers of government in the hands of the federal authorities, and towards the practical confirmation of those prerogatives of supreme overlordship which Congress has been gradually arrogating to itself. The central government is constantly becoming stronger and more active, and Congress is establishing itself as the one sovereign authority in that government. In constitutional theory and in the broader features of past practice, ours has been what Mr. Bagehot has called a "composite" government. Besides state and federal authorities to dispute as to sovereignty, there have been within the federal system itself rival and irreconcilable powers. But gradually the strong are overcoming the weak. If the signs of the times are to be credited, we are fast approaching an adjustment of sovereignty quite as "simple" as need be. Congress is not only to retain the authority it already possesses, but is to be brought again and again face to face with still greater demands upon its energy, its wisdom, and its conscience, is to have ever-widening duties and responsibilities thrust upon it, without being granted a moment's opportunity to look back from the plough to which it has set its hands.

The sphere and influence of national administration and national legislation are widening rapidly. Our populations are growing at such a rate that one's reckoning staggers at counting the possible millions that may have a home and a work on this continent ere fifty more years shall have filled their short span. The East will not always be the centre of national life. The South is fast accumulating wealth, and will faster recover influence. The West has already achieved a greatness which no man can gainsay, and has in store a power of future growth which no man can estimate. Whether these sections are to be harmonious or dissentient depends almost entirely upon the methods and policy of the federal government. If that government be not careful to keep within its own proper sphere and prudent to square its policy by rules of national welfare, sectional lines must and will be known; citizens of one part of the country may look with jealousy and even with hatred upon their fellow-citizens of another part; and faction must tear and dissension distract a country which Providence would bless, but which man may curse. The government of a country so vast and various must be strong, prompt, wieldy, and efficient. Its strength must consist in the certainty and uniformity of its purposes, in its accord with national sentiment, in its unhesitating action, and in its honest aims. It must be steadied and approved by open administration diligently obedient to the more permanent judgments of public opinion; and its only active agency, its representative chambers, must be equipped with something besides abundant powers of legislation.

As at present constituted, the federal government lacks strength because its powers are divided, lacks promptness because its authorities are multiplied, lacks wieldiness because its processes are roundabout, lacks efficiency because its responsibility is indistinct and its action without competent direction. It is a government in which every officer may talk about every other officer's duty without having to render strict account for not doing his own, and in which the masters are held in check and offered contradiction by the servants. Mr. Lowell has called it "government by declamation." Talk is not sobered by any necessity imposed upon those who utter it to suit their actions to their words. There is no day of reckoning for words spoken. The speakers of a congressional majority may, without risk of incurring ridicule or discredit, condemn what their own Committees are doing; and the spokesmen of a minority may urge what contrary courses they please with a well-grounded assurance that what they say will be forgotten before they can be called upon to put it into practice. Nobody stands sponsor for the policy of the government. A dozen men originate it; a dozen compromises twist and alter it; a dozen offices whose names are scarcely known outside of Washington put it into execution.

This is the defect to which, it will be observed, I am constantly recurring; to which I recur again and again because every examination of the system, at whatsoever point begun, leads inevitably to it as to a central secret. It is the defect which interprets all the rest, because it is their common product. It is exemplified in the extraordinary fact that the utterances of the Press have greater weight and are accorded greater credit, though the Press speaks entirely without authority, than the utterances of Congress, though Congress possesses all authority. The gossip of the street is listened to rather than the words of the law-makers. The editor directs public opinion, the congressman obeys it. When a presidential election is at hand, indeed, the words of the political orator gain temporary heed. He is recognized as an authority in the arena, as a professional critic competent to discuss the good and bad points, and to forecast the fortunes of the contestants. There is something definite in hand, and he is known to have studied all its bearings. He is one of the managers, or is thought to be well acquainted with the management. He speaks "from the card." But let him talk, not about candidates, but about measures or about the policy of the government, and his observations sink at once to the level of a mere individual expression of opinion, to which his political occupations seem to add very little weight. It is universally recognized that he speaks without authority, about things which his vote may help to settle, but about which several hundred other men have votes quite as influential as his own. Legislation is not a thing to be known beforehand. It depends upon the conclusions of sundry Standing Committees. It is an aggregate, not a simple, production. It is impossible to tell how many persons' opinions and influences have entered into its composition. It is even impracticable to determine from this year's law-making what next year's will be like.

Speaking, therefore, without authority, the political orator speaks to little purpose when he speaks about legislation. The papers do not report him carefully; and their editorials seldom take any color from his arguments. The Press, being anonymous and representing a large force of inquisitive news-hunters, is much more powerful than he chiefly because it *is* impersonal and seems to represent a wider and more thorough range of information. At the worst, it can easily compete with any ordinary individual. Its individual opinion is quite sure to be esteemed as worthy of attention as any other individual opinion. And, besides, it is almost everywhere strong enough to deny currency to the speeches of individuals whom it does not care to report. It goes to its audience; the orator must depend upon his audience coming to him. It can be heard at every fireside; the orator can be heard only on the platform or the hustings. There is no imperative demand on the part of the reading public in this country that the newspapers should report political speeches in full. On the contrary, most readers would be disgusted at finding their favorite columns so filled up. By giving even a notice of more than an item's length to such a speech, an editor runs the risk of being denounced as dull. And I believe that the position of the American Press is in this regard quite singular. The English newspapers are so far from being thus independent and self-sufficient powers,—a law unto themselves,—in the politics of the empire that they are constrained to do homage to the political orator whether they will or no. Conservative editors must spread before their readers *verbatim* reports not only of the speeches of the leaders of their own party, but also of the principal speeches of the leading Liberal orators; and Liberal journals have no choice but to print every syllable of the more important public utterances of the Conservative leaders. The nation insists upon knowing what its public men have to say, even when it is not so well said as the newspapers which report them could have said it. There are only two things which can give any man a right to expect that when he speaks the whole country will listen: namely, genius and authority. Probably no one will ever contend that Sir Stafford Northcote was an orator, or even a good speaker. But by proof of unblemished character, and by assiduous, conscientious, and able public service he rose to be the recognized leader of his party in the House of Commons; and it is simply because he speaks as one having authority,—and not as the scribes of the Press,—that he is as sure of a heedful hearing as is Mr. Gladstone, who adds genius and noble oratory to the authority of established leadership. The leaders of English public life have something besides weight of character, prestige of personal service and experience, and authority of individual opinion to exalt them above the anonymous Press. They have definite authority and power in the actual control of government. They are directly commissioned to control the policy of the administration. They stand before the country, in parliament and out of it, as the responsible chiefs of their parties. It is their business to lead those parties, and it is the matter-of-course custom of the constituencies to visit upon the parties the punishment due for the mistakes made by these chiefs. They are at once the servants and scapegoats of their parties.

It is these well-established privileges and responsibilities of theirs which make their utterances considered worth hearing, —nay, necessary to be heard and pondered. Their public speeches are their parties' platforms. What the leader promises his party stands ready to do, should it be intrusted with office. This certainty of audience and of credit gives spice to what such leaders have to say, and lends elevation to the tone of all their public utterances. They for the most part avoid buncombe, which would be difficult to translate into Acts of Parliament. It is easy to see how great an advantage their station and influence give them over our own public men. We have no such responsible party leadership on this side the sea; we are very shy about conferring much authority on anybody, and the consequence is that it requires something very like genius to secure for any one of our statesmen a universally recognized right to be heard and to create an ever-active desire to hear him whenever he talks, not about candidates, but about measures. An extraordinary gift of eloquence, such as not every generation may hope to see, will always hold, because it will always captivate, the attention of the people. But genius and eloquence are too rare to be depended upon for the instruction and guidance of the masses; and since our politicians lack the credit of authority and responsibility, they must give place, except at election-time, to the Press, which is everywhere, generally well-informed, and always talking. It is necessarily "government by declamation" and editorial-writing.

It is probably also this lack of leadership which gives to our national parties their curious, conglomerate character. It would seem to be scarcely an exaggeration to say that they are homogeneous only in name. Neither of the two principal parties is of one mind with itself. Each tolerates all sorts of difference of creed and variety of aim within its own ranks. Each pretends to the same purposes and permits among its partisans the same contradictions to those purposes. They are grouped around no legislative leaders whose capacity has been tested and to whose opinions they loyally adhere. They are like armies without officers, engaged upon a campaign which has no great cause at its back. Their names and traditions, not their hopes and policy, keep them together.

It is to this fact, as well as to short terms which allow little time for differences to come to a head, that the easy agreement of congressional majorities should be attributed. In other like assemblies the harmony of majorities is constantly liable to disturbance. Ministers lose their following and find their friends falling away in the midst of a session. But not so in Congress. There, although the majority is frequently simply conglomerate, made up of factions not a few, and bearing in its elements every seed of discord, the harmony of party voting seldom, if ever, suffers an interruption. So far as outsiders can see, legislation generally flows placidly on, and the majority easily has its own way, acting with a sort of matter-of-course unanimity, with no suspicion of individual freedom of action. Whatever revolts may be threatened or accomplished in the ranks of the party outside the House at the polls, its power is never broken inside the House. This is doubtless due in part to the fact that there is no freedom of debate in the House; but there can be no question that it is principally due to the fact that debate is without aim, just because legislation is without consistency. Legislation is conglomerate. The absence of any concert of action amongst the Committees leaves legislation with scarcely any trace of determinate party courses. No two schemes pull together. If there is a coincidence of principle between several bills of the same session, it is generally accidental; and the confusion of policy which prevents intelligent coöperation also, of course, prevents intelligent differences and divisions. There is never a transfer of power from one party to the other during a session, because such a transfer would mean almost nothing. The majority remains of one mind so long as a Congress lives, because its mind is very vaguely ascertained, and its power of planning a split consequently very limited. It has no common mind, and if it had, has not the machinery for changing it. It is led by a score or two of Committees whose composition must remain the same to the end; and who are too numerous, as well as to disconnected, to fight against. It stays on one side because it hardly knows where the boundaries of that side are or how to cross them.

Moreover, there is a certain well-known piece of congressional machinery long ago invented and applied for the special purpose of keeping both majority and minority compact. The legislative caucus has almost as important a part in our system as have the Standing Committees, and deserves as close study as they. Its functions are much more easily understood in all their bearings than those of the Committees, however, because they are much simpler. The caucus is meant as an antidote to the Committees. It is designed to supply the cohesive principle which the multiplicity and mutual independence of the Committees so powerfully tend to destroy. Having no Prime Minister to confer with about the policy of the government, as they see members of parliament doing, our congressmen confer with each other in caucus. Rather than imprudently expose to the world the differences of opinion threatened or developed among its members, each party hastens to remove disrupting debate from the floor of Congress, where the speakers might too hastily commit themselves to insubordination, to quiet conferences behind closed doors, where frightened scruples may be reassured and every disagreement healed with a salve of compromise or subdued with the whip of political expediency. The caucus is the drilling-ground of the party. There its discipline is renewed and strengthened, its uniformity of step and gesture regained. The voting and speaking in the House are generally merely the movements of a sort of dress parade, for which the exercises of the caucus are designed to prepare. It is easy to see how difficult it would be for the party to keep its head amidst the confused cross-movements of the Committees without thus now and again pulling itself together in caucus, where it can ask itself its own mind and pledge itself anew to eternal agreement.

The credit of inventing this device is probably due to the Democrats. They appear to have used it so early as the second session of the eighth Congress. Speaking of that session, a reliable authority says: "During this session of Congress there was far less of free and independent discussion on the measures proposed by the friends of the administration than had been previously practiced in both branches of the national legislature. It appeared that on the most important subjects, the course adopted by the majority was the effect of caucus arrangement, or, in other words, had been previously agreed upon at meetings of the Democratic members held in private. Thus the legislation of Congress was constantly swayed by a party following feelings and pledges rather than according to sound reason or personal conviction." [7] The censure implied in this last sentence may have seemed righteous at the time when such caucus pledges were in disfavor as new-fangled shackles, but it would hardly be accepted as just by the intensely practical politicians of to-day. They would probably prefer to put it thus: That the silvern speech spent in caucus secures the golden silence maintained on the floor of Congress, making each party rich in concord and happy in coöperation.

The fact that makes this defense of the caucus not altogether conclusive is that it is shielded from all responsibility by its sneaking privacy. It has great power without any balancing weight of accountability. Probably its debates would constitute interesting and instructive reading for the public, were they published; but they never get out except in rumors often rehearsed and as often amended. They are, one may take it for granted, much more candid and go much nearer the political heart of the questions discussed than anything that is ever said openly in Congress to the reporters' gallery. They approach matters without masks and handle them without gloves. It might hurt, but it would enlighten us to hear them. As it is, however, there is unhappily no ground for denying their power to override sound reason and personal conviction. The caucus cannot always silence or subdue a large and influential minority of dissentients, but its whip seldom fails to reduce individual malcontents and mutineers into submission. There is no place in congressional jousts for the free lance. The man who disobeys his party caucus is understood to disavow his party allegiance altogether, and to assume that dangerous neutrality which is so apt to degenerate into mere caprice, and which is almost sure to destroy his influence by bringing him under the suspicion of being unreliable,—a suspicion always conclusively damning in practical life. Any individual, or any minority of weak numbers or small influence, who has the temerity to neglect the decisions of the caucus is sure, if the offense be often repeated, or even once committed upon an important issue, to be read out of the party, almost without chance of reinstatement. And every one knows that nothing can be accomplished in politics by mere disagreement. The only privilege such recalcitrants gain is the privilege of disagreement; they are forever shut out from the privilege of confidential coöperation. They have chosen the helplessness of a faction.

It must be admitted, however, that, unfortunate as the necessity is for the existence of such powers as those of the caucus, that necessity actually exists and cannot be neglected. Against the fatal action of so many elements of disintegration it would seem to be imperatively needful that some energetic element of cohesion should be provided. It is doubtful whether in any other nation, with a shorter inheritance of political instinct, parties could long successfully resist the centrifugal forces of the committee system with only the varying attraction of the caucus to detain them. The wonder is that, despite the forcible and unnatural divorcement of legislation and administration and the consequent distraction of legislation from all attention to anything like an intelligent planning and superintendence of policy, we are not cursed with as many factions as now almost hopelessly confuse French politics. That we have had, and continue to have, only two national parties of national importance or real power is fortunate rather than natural. Their names stand for a fact, but scarcely for a reason.

An intelligent observer of our politics[8] has declared that there is in the United States "a class, including thousands and tens of thousands of the best men in the country, who think it possible to enjoy the fruits of good government without working for them." Every one who has seen beyond the outside of our American life must recognize the truth of this; to explain it is to state the sum of all the most valid criticisms of congressional government. Public opinion has no easy vehicle for its judgments, no quick channels for its action. Nothing about the system is direct and simple. Authority is perplexingly subdivided and distributed, and responsibility has to be hunted down in out-of-the-way corners. So that the sum of the whole matter is that the means of working for the fruits of good government are not readily to be found. The average citizen may be excused for esteeming government at best but a haphazard affair, upon which his vote and all of his influence can have but little effect. How is his choice of a representative in Congress to affect the policy of the country as regards the questions in which he is most interested, if the man for whom he votes has no chance of getting on the Standing Committee which has virtual charge of those questions? How is it to make any difference who is chosen President? Has the President any very great authority in matters of vital policy? It seems almost a thing of despair to get any assurance that any vote he may cast will even in an infinitesimal degree affect the essential courses of administration.

There are so many cooks mixing their ingredients in the national broth that it seems hopeless, this thing of changing one cook at a time.

The charm of our constitutional ideal has now been long enough wound up to enable sober men who do not believe in political witchcraft to judge what it has accomplished, and is likely still to accomplish, without further winding. The Constitution is not honored by blind worship. The more open-eyed we become, as a nation, to its defects, and the prompter we grow in applying with the unhesitating courage of conviction all thoroughly-tested or well-considered expedients necessary to make self-government among us a straightforward thing of simple method, single, unstinted power, and clear responsibility, the nearer will we approach to the sound sense and practical genius of the great and honorable statesmen of 1787. And the first step towards emancipation from the timidity and false pride which have led us to seek to thrive despite the defects of our national system rather than seem to deny its perfection is a fearless criticism of that system. When we shall have examined all its parts without sentiment, and gauged all its functions by the standards of practical common sense, we shall have established anew our right to the claim of political sagacity; and it will remain only to act intelligently upon what our opened eyes have seen in order to prove again the justice of our claim to political genius.

SOURCES TO INTRODUCTION BY
WALTER LIPPMANN

CONS G—*Constitutional Government in the United States,*
  eighth printing, 1947.
B— Ray Stannard Baker, *Woodrow Wilson, Life and
  Letters,* Vol. I.
PP— *The Public Papers of Woodrow Wilson,* edited by
  Ray Stannard Baker and William E. Dodd, Harper
  & Brothers, Vol. I, 1925.
BAG— Walter Bagehot, *The English Constitution and
  Other Political Essays,* D. Appleton and Com-
  pany, 1914.

NOTES

INTRODUCTION BY WALTER LIPPMANN

[1] B 154.
[2] B 103.
[3] B 105.
[4] p. 91.
[5] p. 37.
[6] B 96.
[7] B 213.
[8] BAG 52 *et seq.*
[9] CG 43.
[10] p. 95.
[11] CG 315.
[12] CG 42.
[13] CG 52.
[14] CG 45.
[15] p. 95.
[16] p. 114.
[17] p. 41.
[18] CONS G 67 *et seq.*

PREFACE TO FIFTEENTH PRINTING

[1] These are Mr. Bagehot's words with reference to the British constitutional system. See his *English Constitution* (last American
edition), p. 69.
[2] *Works*, vol. vi., p. 467: "Letter to Jno. Taylor." The words and
sentences omitted in the quotation contain Mr. Adams's opinions

as to the value of the several balances, some of which he thinks of doubtful utility, and others of which he, without hesitation, pronounces altogether pernicious.

[3] *Federalist,* No. 17.

[4] Cooley's *Principles of Constitutional Law,* p. 143.

[5] McMaster, *Hist. of the People of the U. S.,* vol. i., p. 564.

[6] Lodge's *Alexander Hamilton* (Am. Statesmen Series), p. 85.

[7] Lodge's *Alexander Hamilton,* p. 105.

[8] Its final and most masterly exposition, by C. J. Marshall, may be seen in McCulloch v. Maryland, 4 Wheaton, 316.

[9] The following passage from William Maclay's *Sketches of Debate in the First Senate of the United States* (pp. 292-293) illustrates how clearly the results of this were forecast by sagacious men from the first: "The system laid down by these gentlemen (the Federalists) was as follows, or rather the development of the designs of a certain party: The general power to carry the Constitution into effect by a constructive interpretation would extend to every case that Congress may deem necessary or expedient. . . . The laws of the United States will be held paramount to all" state "laws, claims, and even constitutions. The supreme power is with the general government to decide in this, as in everything else, for the States have neglected to secure any umpire or mode of decision in case of difference between them. Nor is there any point in the Constitution for them to rally under. They may give an opinion, but the opinions of the general government must prevail. . . . Any direct and open act would be termed usurpation. But whether the gradual influence and encroachments of the general government may not gradually swallow up the state governments, is another matter."

[10] Pensacola Tel. Co. v. West. Union, 96 U. S. 1, 9. (Quoted by Judge Cooley in his *Principles of Constitutional Law.*)

[11] 18 Stat., part 3, 336. See Ex parte Virginia, 100 U. S. 339.

[12] Sect. 5515 Rev. Stats. See Ex parte Siebold, 100 U. S. 371. Equally extensive of federal powers is that "legal tender" decision (Juilliard v. Greenman) of March, 1884, which argues the existence of a right to issue an irredeemable paper currency from the Constitution's grant of other rights characteristic of sovereignty, and from the possession of a similar right by other governments. But this involves no restriction of state powers; and perhaps there ought to be offset against it that other decision (several cases, October, 1883), which denies constitutional sanction to the Civil Rights Act.

[13] *Principles of Constitutional Law,* pp. 143, 144.

[14] Marbury v. Madison, 1 Cranch, 137.

[15] Cooley's *Principles,* p. 157.

[16] For an incisive account of the whole affair, see an article entitled "The Session," *North American Review,* vol. cxi., pp. 48, 49.

[17] 7 Wall. 506.

[18] For a brilliant account of the senatorial history of these two treaties, see the article entitled "The Session," *North American Rev.,* vol. cviii. (1869), p. 626 *et seq.*

THE HOUSE OF REPRESENTATIVES

[1] In an article entitled "The Conduct of Business in Congress" (*North American Review,* vol. cxxviii., p. 113), to which I am indebted for many details of the sketch in the text.

[2] No Committee is entitled, when called, to occupy more than the morning hours of two successive days with the measures which it has prepared; though if its second morning hour expire while the House is actually considering one of its bills, that single measure may hold over from morning hour to morning hour until it is disposed of.

[3] Quoted from an exceedingly life-like and picturesque description of the House which appeared in the New York *Nation* for April 4, 1878.

[4] *North American Review,* vol. xxvi., p. 162.

[5] *Id.,* the same article.

[6] "Glances at Congress," *Democratic Review,* March, 1839.

[7] *Autobiography,* pp. 264, 265.

THE HOUSE OF REPRESENTATIVES
Revenue and Supply

[1] *The National Budget, etc.* (English Citizen Series), p. 146. In what I have to say of the English system, I follow this volume, pp. 146-149, and another volume of the same admirable series, entitled *Central Government,* pp. 36-47, most of my quotations being from the latter.

[2] See an article entitled "National Appropriations and Misappropriations," by the late President Garfield, *North American Review,* vol. cxxviii., pp. 578 *et seq.*

[3] Senator Hoar's article, already several times quoted.

[4] Adams's *John Randolph.* American Statesman Series, pp. 210, 211.

[5] On one occasion "the House passed thirty-seven pension bills at one sitting. The Senate, on its part, by unanimous consent, took up and passed in about ten minutes seven bills providing for public buildings in different States, appropriating an aggregate of $1,200,000 in this short time. A recent House feat was one in which a bill, allowing 1,300 war claims in a lump, was passed. It contained one hundred and nineteen pages full of little claims, amounting in all to $291,000; and a member, in deprecating criticism on this disposition of them, said that the Committee had

received ten huge bags full of such claims, which had been adjudicated by the Treasury officials, and it was a physical impossibility to examine them."—*N. Y. Sun,* 1881.

[6] Congress, though constantly erecting new Committees, never gives up old ones, no matter how useless they may have become by subtraction of duties. Thus there is not only the superseded Committee on Public Expenditures but the Committee on Manufacturers also, which, when a part of the one-time Committee on Commerce and Manufacturers, had plenty to do, but which, since the creation of a distinct Committee on Commerce, has had nothing to do, having now, together with the Committees on Agriculture and Indian Affairs, no duties assigned to it by the rules. It remains to be seen whether the Committee on Commerce will suffer a like eclipse because of the gift of its principal duties to the new Committee on Rivers and Harbors.

[7] See the report of this Committee, which was under the chairmanship of Senator Windom.

An illustration of what the House Committees find by special effort may be seen in the revelations of the investigation of the expenses of the notorious "Star Route Trials" made by the Forty-eighth Congress's Committee on Expenditures in the Department of Justice.

[8] See General Garfield's article, already once quoted, *North American Review,* vol. cxxviii., p. 583.

[9] *Essays on Parliamentary Reform.*

[10] Green's *History of the English People,* vol. iv., pp. 202, 203.

[11] "G. B." in N. Y. *Nation,* Nov. 30, 1882.

THE SENATE

[1] An attempt was once made to bring the previous question into the practices of the Senate, but it failed of success, and so that imperative form of cutting off all further discussion has fortunately never found a place there.

[2] As regards all financial measures indeed committee supervision is specially thorough in the Senate. "All amendments to general appropriation bills reported from the Committees of the Senate, proposing new items of appropriation, shall, one day before they are offered, be referred to the Committee on Appropriations, and all general appropriation bills shall be referred to said Committee; and in like manner amendments to bills making appropriations for rivers and harbors shall be again referred to the Committee to which such bills shall be referred."—Senate Rule 30.

[3] The twenty-nine Standing Committees of the Senate are, however, chosen by ballot, not appointed by the Vice-President, who is an appendage, not a member, of the Senate.

[4] In the Birmingham Town Hall, November 3, 1882. I quote from the report of the *London Times.*

[5] "No Senator shall speak more than twice, in any one debate, on the same day, without leave of the Senate."—Senate Rule 4.

[6] These quotations from Bagehot are taken from various parts of the fifth chapter of his *English Constitution.*

[7] These are the words of Lord Rosebery—testimony from the oldest and most celebrated second chamber that exists.

[8] There seems to have been at one time a tendency towards a better practice. In 1813 the Senate sought to revive the early custom, in accordance with which the President delivered his messages in person, by requesting the attendance of the President to consult upon foreign affairs; but Mr. Madison declined.

[9] *North American Review,* vol. 108, p. 625.

THE EXECUTIVE

[1] *English Constitution,* chap. viii., p. 293.

[2] *Atlantic Monthly,* vol. xxv., p. 148.

[3] Something like this has been actually proposed by Mr. Albert Stickney, in his interesting and incisive essay, *A True Republic.*

[4] State, Treasury, War, Navy.

[5] As quoted in *Macmillan's Magazine,* vol. vii., p. 67.

[6] I quote from an excellent handbook, *The United States Government,* by Lamphere.

[7] "In America the President cannot prevent any law from being passed, nor can he evade the obligation of enforcing it. His sincere and zealous coöperation is no doubt useful, but it is not indispensable, in the carrying on of public affairs. All his important acts are directly or indirectly submitted to the legislature, and of his own free authority he can do but little. It is, therefore, his weakness, and not his power, which enables him to remain in opposition to Congress. In Europe, harmony must reign between the Crown and the other branches of the legislature, because a collision between them may prove serious; in America, this harmony is not indispensable, because such a collision is impossible."
—De Tocqueville, i., p. 124.

[8] *Westminster Review,* vol. lxvi., p. 193.

[9] Tenure of Office Act, already discussed.

[10] These "ifs" are abundantly supported by the executive acts of the war-time. The Constitution had then to stand aside that President Lincoln might be as prompt as the seeming necessities of the time.

[11] *Central Government* (Eng. Citizen Series), H. D. Traill, p. 20.

CONCLUSION

[1] Professor Sumner's *Andrew Jackson* (American Statesmen Series), p. 226. "Finally," adds Prof. S., "the methods and machinery of democratic republican self-government—caucuses, primaries, committees, and conventions—lend themselves perhaps more easily than any other methods and machinery to the uses of selfish cliques which seek political influence for interested purposes."

[2] Bagehot: *Essay on Sir Robert Peel*, p. 24.

[3] H. C. Lodge's *Alexander Hamilton* (Am. Statesmen Series), pp. 60, 61.

[4] Bagehot, *Eng. Const.*, p. 293.

[5] Bagehot, *Eng. Const.*, p. 296.

[6] Green: *Hist. of the English People* (Harper's ed.), iv., pp. 58, 59.

[7] *Statesman's Manual*, i., p. 244.

[8] Mr. Dale, of Birmingham.

Woodrow Wilson

Woodrow (Thomas) Wilson was born in Staunton, Va. on December 28, 1856 and died on February 3, 1924. Twenty-eighth President of the United States, educator, and historian, he was a lifelong student of political theory and the realities underlying political organization. His published works include, in addition to numerous papers, *Constitutional Government in the United States; Division and Reunion; George Washington;* and *A History of the American People.*